Amazon AppStream 2.0 Developer Guide

A catalogue record for this book is available from the Hong Kong Public Libraries.

Published in Hong Kong by Samurai Media Limited.

Email: info@samuraimedia.org

ISBN 9789888408665

Contents

What Is Amazon AppStream 2.0?

Amazon AppStream 2.0 is a fully managed application streaming service that provides users with instant access to their desktop applications from anywhere. AppStream 2.0 manages the AWS resources required to host and run your applications, scales automatically, and provides access to your users on demand. AppStream 2.0 provides users access to the applications they need on the desktop device of their choice, with a responsive, fluid user experience that is indistinguishable from natively installed applications. There are no files to download and no time-consuming installations.

With AppStream 2.0, you can easily add your existing desktop applications to AWS and instantly start streaming them to an HTML5 compatible browser. You can maintain a single version of each of your applications, which makes application management easier. Your users always access the latest versions of their applications. Your applications run on AWS compute resources, and data is never stored on users' devices, which means they always get a high performance, secure experience.

Unlike traditional on-premises solutions for desktop application streaming, AppStream 2.0 offers pay-as-you-go pricing, with no upfront investment and no infrastructure to maintain. You can scale instantly and globally, ensuring that your users always have the best possible experience.

For more information, see AppStream 2.0.

Features

Using Amazon AppStream 2.0 provides the following advantages:

Run desktop applications securely on any desktop device
Your desktop applications run securely in an HTML5 web browser on Windows and Linux PCs, Macs, and Chromebooks.

Secure applications and data
Applications and data remain on AWS — only encrypted pixels are streamed to end users. Applications run on an AppStream 2.0 instance dedicated to each user so that compute resources are not shared. Applications can run inside your own virtual private cloud (VPC), and you can use Amazon VPC security features to control access. This enables you to isolate your applications and deliver them in a secure way.

Consistent, scalable performance
AppStream 2.0 runs on AWS with access to compute capabilities not available on local devices, which means that your applications run with consistently high performance. You can instantly scale locally and globally, and ensure that your users always get a low-latency experience. Unlike on-premises solutions, you can quickly deploy your applications to the AWS region that is closest to your users, and start streaming with no incremental capital investment.

Integrate with your IT environment
Integrate with your existing AWS services and your on-premises environments. By running applications inside your VPCs, your users can access data and other resources that you have in AWS. This reduces the movement of data between AWS and your environment and provides a faster user experience.
Integrate with your existing Microsoft Active Directory environment. This enables you to use existing Active Directory governance, user experience, and security policies with your streaming applications.
Configure identity federation, which allows your users to access their applications using their corporate credentials. You can also allow authenticated access to your IT resources from applications running on AppStream 2.0.

Choose the fleet type that meets your needs
There are two types of fleets:

- Always-On — Your instances run all the time, even when no users are streaming applications. Use an Always-On fleet to provide your users with instant access to their applications.

- On-Demand — Your instances run only when users are streaming applications. Idle instances that are available for streaming are in a stopped state. Use an On-Demand fleet to optimize your streaming charges and provide your users with access to their applications after a 1-2 minute wait. For more information, see Amazon AppStream 2.0 Pricing.

Key Concepts

To get the most out of AppStream 2.0, be familiar with the following concepts:

image builder
An *image builder* is a virtual machine that you use to create an image. You can launch and connect to an image builder by using the AWS Management Console. After you are connected to an image builder, you can install, add, and test your apps, and then use the image builder to publish an image.

image
An *image* contains applications that are streamed to users. AWS provides base images that you can use to create images that include your own applications.

fleet
A *fleet* consists of streaming instances that run the image that you specify. You can set the desired number of streaming instances for your fleet and configure policies to scale your fleet automatically based on demand. Note that one user requires one instance.

stack
A *stack* consists of an associated fleet, user access policies, and storage configurations. You set up a stack to start streaming applications to users.

user pool
Use the *user pool* to manage users and their assigned stacks.

How to Get Started

If you are using AppStream 2.0 for the first time, you can use the **Try it Now **feature or follow the Getting Started with Amazon AppStream 2.0 tutorial (both are available in the AppStream 2.0 console).

- **Try It Now **provides you with a free trial experience that allows you to easily start desktop applications from your desktop browser.

- The Getting Started tutorial enables you to set up application streaming by using sample applications or your own applications. If you decide to start by using sample applications, you can always add your own applications later.

  For more information about these two options, see Amazon AppStream 2.0 FAQs.

When you use the service for the first time, AppStream 2.0 creates an AWS Identity and Access Management (IAM) role to create and manage AppStream 2.0 resources on your behalf.

To use the Try It Now feature

1. Open the AppStream 2.0 console at https://console.aws.amazon.com/appstream2.

2. Choose **Try it now**.

3. Sign in using your AWS account credentials, if requested.

4. Read the terms and conditions and choose **Agree and Continue**.

5. From the list of applications shown, select one to try.

To run the Getting Started tutorial

1. Open the AppStream 2.0 console at https://console.aws.amazon.com/appstream2.

2. Choose **Get Started**.

3. Select the option to learn more about AppStream 2.0 resources.

Accessing AppStream 2.0

You can work with AppStream 2.0 using any of the following interfaces:

AWS Management Console
The console is a browser-based interface to manage AppStream 2.0 resources. For more information, see Getting Started with Amazon AppStream 2.0.

AWS command line tools
AWS provides two sets of command line tools: the AWS Command Line Interface (AWS CLI) and the AWS Tools for Windows PowerShell. To use the AWS CLI to run AppStream 2.0 commands, see Amazon AppStream 2.0 Command Line Reference.

AWS SDKs
You can access AppStream 2.0 from a variety of programming languages. The SDKs automatically take care of tasks such as the following:

- Setting up an AppStream 2.0 stack or fleet
- Getting an application streaming URL to your stack
- Describing your resources For more information, see Tools for Amazon Web Services.

Setting Up for Amazon AppStream 2.0

Complete the following tasks to get set up for Amazon AppStream 2.0.

Sign Up for AWS

When you sign up for AWS, your AWS account is automatically signed up for all services, including AppStream 2.0. You are charged only for the services that you use.

If you have an AWS account already, skip to the next task. If you don't have an AWS account, use the following procedure to create one.

To create an AWS account

1. Open https://aws.amazon.com/, and then choose **Create an AWS Account. Note**
   This might be unavailable in your browser if you previously signed into the AWS Management Console. In that case, choose **Sign in to a different account**, and then choose **Create a new AWS account**.

2. Follow the online instructions.

   Part of the sign-up procedure involves receiving a phone call and entering a PIN using the phone keypad.

Getting Started with Amazon AppStream 2.0

To stream your applications, Amazon AppStream 2.0 requires an environment that includes a fleet that is associated with a stack, and at least one application image. This tutorial describes how to configure a sample AppStream 2.0 environment for application streaming and give users access to that stream.

Note
For additional guidance in learning how to get started with AppStream 2.0, see the Amazon AppStream 2.0 Getting Started Guide. This guide describes how to install and configure two applications, perform foundational administrative tasks using the AppStream 2.0 console, and provision an Amazon Virtual Private Cloud by using a provided AWS CloudFormation template.

Topics

- Step 1: Set Up a Sample Stack, Choose an Image, and Configure a Fleet
- Step 2: Provide Access to Users
- Resources

Step 1: Set Up a Sample Stack, Choose an Image, and Configure a Fleet

Before you can stream your applications, you need to set up a stack, choose an image that has applications installed, and configure a fleet. In this step, you use a template to help simplify these tasks.

To set up a sample stack, choose an image, and configure a fleet

1. Open the AppStream 2.0 console at https://console.aws.amazon.com/appstream2.

2. Choose **Get Started** if you are new to the console, or **Quick Links** from the left navigation menu. Choose **Set up with sample apps**.

3. For **Step 1: Stack Details**, keep the default stack name or enter your own. Optionally, you can provide the following:

    - **Display name** — Enter a name to display for the stack (maximum of 100 characters).
    - **Description**— Keep the default description or enter your own (maximum of 256 characters).
    - **Redirect URL** — Specify a URL to which users are redirected after their streaming sessions end.
    - **Feedback URL** — Specify a URL to which users are redirected after they click the Send Feedback link to submit feedback about their application streaming experience. If you do not specify a URL, this link is not displayed.

4. Choose **Next**.

5. For **Step 2: Choose Image**, choose an image, and then choose **Next**. The sample image contains pre-installed open source applications for evaluation purposes. For more information, see Amazon AppStream 2.0 Windows Image Version History.

6. For **Step 3: Configure Fleet**, we recommend that you keep the default values and choose **Next**. You can change most of these values after fleet creation.

    - **Choose instance type** — Choose the instance type that matches the performance requirements of your applications. All streaming instances in your fleet launch with the instance type that you select. For more information, see AppStream 2.0 Instance Families.

    - **Fleet type** — Choose the fleet type that suits your use case. The fleet type determines its immediate availability and how you pay for it.

    - **Maximum session duration** — Choose the maximum amount of time that a streaming session can remain active. If users are still connected to a streaming session five minutes before this limit is reached, they are prompted to save any open documents before being disconnected.

- **Disconnect timeout** — Choose the time that a streaming instance should remain active after users disconnect. If users try to reconnect to the streaming session after a disconnection or network interruption within this time interval, they are connected to the previous session. Otherwise, they are connected to a new session with a new instance. If you associate a stack with a fleet for which a redirect URL is specified, after users' streaming sessions end, the users are redirected to that URL.

  If a user ends the session by choosing **End Session** on the streaming session toolbar, the disconnect timeout does not apply. Instead, the user is prompted to save any open documents, and then immediately disconnected from the streaming instance.

- **Minimum capacity** — Choose a minimum number of instances for your fleet based on the minimum number of expected concurrent users. Every unique user session is served by an instance. For example, to have your stack support 100 concurrent users during low demand, specify a minimum capacity of 100. This ensures that 100 instances are running even if there are fewer than 100 users.

- **Maximum capacity** — Choose a maximum number of instances for your fleet based on the maximum number of expected concurrent users. Every unique user session is served by an instance. For example, to have your stack support 500 concurrent users during high demand, specify a maximum capacity of 500. This ensures that up to 500 instances can be created on demand.

7. For **Step 4: Configure Network**, choose a VPC and two subnets with access to the network resources that your application needs, and then choose **Next**. If you don't have a VPC or subnets, you can create them using the links provided and then click the refresh icons. For **Security groups**, you can select up to five security groups. Otherwise, the default security group is used. For more information, see Network Settings for Amazon AppStream 2.0 .

8. For **Step 5: Enable Storage**, do the following, then choose **Next**.

   - **Enable Home Folders** — By default, this setting is enabled. Keep the default setting. For information about requirements for enabling home folders, see Enable Home Folders for Your AppStream 2.0 Users.
   - **Enable Google Drive** — Optionally, you can also enable users to link their Google Drive account to AppStream 2.0. You can enable Google Drive for accounts in G Suite domains only, not for personal Gmail accounts. For information about requirements for enabling Google Drive, see Enable Google Drive for Your AppStream 2.0 Users.

9. For **Step 6: User Settings**, select the ways in which your users can transfer data between their streaming session and their local device. When you're done, choose **Review**:

   - **Clipboard** — By default, users can copy and paste data between their local device and streaming applications. You can limit Clipboard options so that users can paste data to their remote streaming session only or copy data to their local device only, or you can disable Clipboard options entirely. Note that users can still copy and paste between applications in their streaming session.
   - **File transfer** — By default, users can upload and download files between their local device and streaming session. You can limit file transfer options so that users can upload files to their streaming session only or download files to their local device only, or you can disable file transfer entirely.
   - **Print to local device** — By default, users can print to their local device from within a streaming application. When they choose **Print** in the application, they can download a .pdf file that they can print to a local printer. You can disable this option to prevent users from printing to a local device. **Note**
     These settings affect only whether users can use AppStream 2.0 data transfer features. If your image provides access to a browser, network printer, or other remote resource, your users might be able to transfer data to or from their streaming session in other ways.

10. For **Step 7: Review**, confirm the details for the stack. To change the configuration for any section, choose **Edit **and make the needed changes. After you finish reviewing the configuration details, choose **Create**.

11. After the service sets up resources, the **Stacks** page appears. The status of your new stack appears as

Active when it is ready to use.

Optionally, you can apply one or more tags to help manage the stack. Choose **Tags**, choose **Add/Edit Tags**, choose **Add Tag**, specify the key and value for the tag, and then choose **Save**. For more information, see Tagging Your Amazon AppStream 2.0 Resources.

Step 2: Provide Access to Users

After you create a stack, each user needs an active URL for access. The AppStream 2.0 User Pool feature enables you to create and manage users, using a permanent login portal URL. For more information, see Manage Access Using the AppStream 2.0 User Pool. To quickly test application streaming without setting up users, create a temporary URL as shown below.

To provide access to users with a temporary URL

1. In the navigation pane, choose **Stacks**. Select the radio button for the stack, and then choose **Actions, Create Streaming URL**.

2. For **User id**, type the user ID. Select an expiration time, which determines how long the generated URL is valid.

3. To view the user ID and URL, choose **Get URL**.

4. To copy the link to the clipboard, choose **Copy Link**.

Resources

For more information, see the following:

- Learn how to use the AppStream 2.0 image builder to add your own applications and create images that you can stream to your users. For more information, see Tutorial: Create a Custom Image.
- Provide persistent storage for your session users by using AppStream 2.0 home folders and Google Drive. For more information, see Enable Persistent Storage for Your AppStream 2.0 Users.
- Integrate your AppStream 2.0 streaming resources with your Microsoft Active Directory environment. For more information, see Using Active Directory with AppStream 2.0.
- Control who has access to your AppStream 2.0 streaming instances. For more information, see Controlling Access to Amazon AppStream 2.0 with IAM Policies and Service Roles, Manage Access Using the AppStream 2.0 User Pool and Single Sign-on Access to AppStream 2.0 Using SAML 2.0.
- Monitor your AppStream 2.0 resources by using Amazon CloudWatch. For more information, see AppStream 2.0 Metrics and Dimensions.
- Troubleshoot your AppStream 2.0 streaming experience. For more information, see Troubleshooting.

Network Settings for Amazon AppStream 2.0

The following sections contain information about enabling users to connnect to AppStream 2.0 streaming instances and enabling your AppStream 2.0 fleets and image builders to access network resources and the internet.

Contents

Network Setup Guidelines

There are some network setup guidelines to consider for fleets and image builders. If your fleets and image builders require internet access, you can use the Default Internet Access feature. You could also manually control internet access using an advanced networking configuration, such as a VPC with NAT gateways. For more information, see Enabling Internet Access Using a Public Subnet and Enabling Internet Access Using a NAT Gateway.

Fleets

You can provide subnets to establish network connections from your fleet instances to your VPC. We recommend that you specify two private subnets from different Availability Zones for high availability and fault tolerance. Also, ensure that the network resources for your applications are accessible through both of the specified private subnets.

AppStream 2.0 creates as many elastic network interfaces as the maximum desired capacity of your fleet. The following guidelines will help you set up a VPC to support scaling behavior for your fleet.

- Make sure that your AWS account has sufficient elastic network interface capacity to support the scaling requirements of your fleet. If you are planning to launch a large fleet of streaming instances, contact AWS Support and request a higher ENI limit to match the maximum number of instances that you plan to launch.
- Specify subnets with a sufficient number of elastic IP addresses to match the maximum desired capacity of your fleet.
- Use security groups to provide your VPC with specific security settings. For more information, see Security Groups.

15

Image Builders

You can choose one subnet while launching an image builder. Ensure the subnet accessibility of the network resources, with which your applications may interact. The typical resources required for the successful execution of your apps may include licensing servers, database servers, file servers, and so on.

Security Groups

You can provide additional access control to your VPC from streaming instances in a fleet or an image builder in Amazon AppStream 2.0 by associating them with VPC security groups. Security groups that belong to your VPC allow you to control the network traffic between AppStream 2.0 streaming instances and VPC resources such as license servers, file servers, and database servers. For more information, see Security Groups for your VPC in the *Amazon VPC User Guide*.

The rules that you define for your VPC security group are applied when the security group is associated with a fleet or image builder. The security group rules determine what network traffic is allowed from your streaming instances. For more information, see Security Group Rules in the *Amazon VPC User Guide*.

You can associate up to five security groups while launching a new image builder or while creating a new fleet. You can also associate security groups to an existing fleet or change the security groups of a fleet. For more information, see Working with Security Groups in the *Amazon VPC User Guide*.

If you don't select a security group, your image builder or fleet is associated with the default security group for your VPC. For more information, see Default Security Group for Your VPC in the *Amazon VPC User Guide*.

Use these additional considerations when using security groups with AppStream 2.0.

- All end user data, such as internet traffic, Home folder data, or application communication with VPC resources, are affected by the security groups associated with the streaming instance.
- Streaming pixel data is not affected by security groups.
- If you have enabled default internet access for your fleet or image builder, the rules of the associated security groups must allow internet access.

You can create or edit rules for your security groups or create new security groups using the Amazon VPC console.

- **To associate security groups with an image builder** — Follow the instructions at Step 1: Create an Image Builder.
- **To associate security groups with a fleet**
  - *While creating the fleet* — Follow the instructions at Create a Fleet.
  - *For an existing fleet* — Edit the fleet settings using the AWS Management Console.

You can also associate security groups to your fleets using the AWS CLI and SDKs.

- **AWS CLI** — Use the create-fleet and update-fleet commands.
- **AWS SDKs** — Use the CreateFleet and UpdateFleet API operations.

For more information, see the AWS Command Line Interface User Guide and Tools for Amazon Web Services.

Home Folders and VPC Endpoints

To support home folders on a private network, AppStream 2.0 needs access permissions to the VPC endpoint. To enable AppStream 2.0 access to your private Amazon S3 endpoint, attach a custom policy, as defined below, to your VPC endpoint for Amazon S3. For more information about private Amazon S3 endpoints, see VPC Endpoints and Endpoints for Amazon S3 in the *Amazon VPC User Guide*.

```
1 {
2   "Version": "2012-10-17",
```

```
 3   "Statement": [
 4     {
 5       "Sid": "Allow-AppStream-to-access-specific-bucket",
 6       "Effect": "Allow",
 7       "Principal": {
 8         "AWS": "arn:aws:sts::account-id-without-hyphens:assumed-role/
               AmazonAppStreamServiceAccess/AppStream2.0"
 9       },
10       "Action": [
11         "s3:ListBucket",
12         "s3:GetObject",
13         "s3:PutObject",
14         "s3:DeleteObject",
15         "s3:GetObjectVersion",
16         "s3:DeleteObjectVersion"
17       ],
18       "Resource": "arn:aws:s3:::appstream2-36fb080bb8-*"
19     }
20   ]
21 }
```

Port Requirements for User Connections to Amazon AppStream 2.0

For AppStream 2.0 users to connect to streaming instances and stream applications, the network that the users' devices are connected to must allow access to certain IP addresses and ports.

Ports for AppStream 2.0 User Devices

AppStream 2.0 users' devices require outbound access on port 443 (TCP), and if you are using DNS servers for domain name resolution, port 53 (UDP).

- Port 443 is used for HTTPS communication between AppStream 2.0 users' devices and streaming instances. Typically, when end users browse the web during streaming sessions, the web browser randomly selects a source port in the high range for streaming traffic. You must ensure that return traffic to this port is allowed.
- Port 53 is used for communication between AppStream 2.0 users' devices and your DNS servers. The port must be open to the IP addresses for your DNS servers so that public domain names can be resolved. This port is optional if you are not using DNS servers for domain name resolution.

Whitelisted Domains

For AppStream 2.0 users to access streaming instances, you must whitelist the following domains on the network from which users are trying to access the streaming instances.

- Session Gateway: *.amazonappstream.com
- CloudFront: *.cloudfront.net

Amazon Web Services (AWS) publishes its current IP address ranges, including the ranges that the Session Gateway and CloudFront domains may resolve to, in JSON format. For information about how to download the .json file and view the current ranges, see AWS IP Address Ranges in the Amazon Web Services General Reference. Or, if you are using AWS Tools for Windows PowerShell, you can access the same information by using the `Get-AWSPublicIpAddressRange` cmdlet. For more information, see Querying the Public IP Address Ranges for AWS.

Port Requirements for Amazon AppStream 2.0 Connections to Network Resources and the Internet

To enable AppStream 2.0 connectivity to network resources and the internet, configure your streaming instances as follows.

Network Interfaces

Each AppStream 2.0 streaming instance has the following network interfaces:

- The customer network interface provides connectivity to the resources within your VPC, as well as the internet, and is used to join the streaming instance to your directory.
- The management network interface is connected to a secure AppStream 2.0 management network. It is used for interactive streaming of the streaming instance to a user's device, and to allow AppStream 2.0 to manage the streaming instance.

AppStream 2.0 selects the IP address for the management network interface from the following private IP address range: 198.19.0.0/16. Do not use this range for your VPC CIDR or peer your VPC with another VPC with this range, as this might create a conflict and cause streaming instances to be unreachable. Also, do not modify or delete any of the network interfaces attached to a streaming instance, as this might also cause the streaming instance to become unreachable.

Management Network Interface IP Address Range and Ports

The management network interface IP address range is 198.19.0.0/16. The following ports must be open on the management network interface of all streaming instances:

- Inbound TCP on port 8300. This is used for establishment of the streaming connection.
- Inbound TCP on port 8443. This is used for management of the streaming instance by AppStream 2.0.

Limit the inbound range on the management network interface to 198.19.0.0/16.

Under normal circumstances, AppStream 2.0 correctly configures these ports for your streaming instances. If any security or firewall software is installed on a streaming instance that blocks any of these ports, the streaming instance may not function correctly or may be unreachable.

Customer Network Interface Ports

- For internet connectivity, the following ports must be open to all destinations. If you are using a modified or custom security group, you need to add the required rules manually. For more information, see Security Group Rules in the *Amazon VPC User Guide*.

  - TCP 80 (HTTP)
  - TCP 443 (HTTPS)

- If you join your streaming instances to a directory, the following ports must be open between your AppStream 2.0 VPC and your directory controllers.

  - TCP/UDP 53 - DNS
  - TCP/UDP 88 - Kerberos authentication
  - UDP 123 - NTP
  - TCP 135 - RPC
  - UDP 137-138 - Netlogon
  - TCP 139 - Netlogon
  - TCP/UDP 389 - LDAP

- TCP/UDP 445 - SMB
- TCP 1024-65535 - Dynamic ports for RPC

For a complete list of ports, see Active Directory and Active Directory Domain Services Port Requirements in the Microsoft documentation.

- All streaming instances require that port 80 (HTTP) be open to IP address 169.254.169.254 to allow access to the EC2 metadata service. Any HTTP proxy assigned to your streaming instances must exclude 169.254.169.254.

Enabling Internet Access Using a Public Subnet

AppStream 2.0 can provide your fleets with a default internet connection by using your Amazon VPC public subnet. This subnet has a route to the internet through an internet gateway.

AppStream 2.0 enables internet connectivity by associating an Elastic IP address to the network interface that is attached from the streaming instance to your VPC public subnet. You can have a VPC with a public subnet in several ways:

Default VPC
Your AWS account, if it was created after 2013-12-04, has a default VPC that has public subnets. You can use this default VPC to enable internet access from your streaming instances. For more information, see Default VPC and Default Subnets in the *Amazon VPC User Guide*.

New VPC
If your AWS account was created before 2013-12-04 or to manage a new VPC, you can create a new VPC with a public subnet using the VPC creation wizard. For more information, see Implementation of VPC with a single public subnet in the *Amazon VPC User Guide*.

Existing VPC
To use an existing VPC that does not have a public subnet, you can add a new public subnet using the following steps.

To add a new public subnet to an existing VPC

1. Follow the steps in Creating a Subnet in the *Amazon VPC User Guide*, using the existing VPC you intend to use with AppStream 2.0.

2. To add an internet gateway to your VPC, follow the steps in Attaching an Internet Gateway in the *Amazon VPC User Guide*.

3. To configure your subnets to route internet traffic through the internet gateway, follow the steps in Creating a Custom Route Table in the *Amazon VPC User Guide*. Use IPv4 format (0.0.0.0/0) for **Destination**.

Enabling Internet Access for a Fleet

After you have a public subnet available on a VPC, you can enable internet access for your fleet. This can be performed either when you create the fleet, or by editing the fleet details after creation.

To enable internet access at fleet creation

1. Follow the instructions at Create a Fleet up to the **Network access** section.

2. Choose **Default Internet Access**.

3. If the subnet fields are empty, select a subnet for **Subnet 1** and, if desired, **Subnet 2**.

4. Continue with the instructions at Create a Fleet.

To enable internet access after fleet creation

1. In the navigation pane, choose **Fleets**.

2. Select a fleet and check that its state is **Stopped**.

3. Choose **Fleet Details, Edit, Default Internet Access**.

4. Choose a subnet for **Subnet 1** and, if desired, **Subnet 2**. Choose **Update**.

You can test internet connectivity by starting your fleet, creating a stack, associating the fleet to a stack, and browsing the internet within a streaming session for stack. For more information, see Create AppStream 2.0 Fleets and Stacks.

Enabling Internet Access for an Image Builder

After you have a public subnet available on a VPC, and can enable internet access for your image builder. This can be performed when you create the image builder.

To enable internet access for an image builder

1. Follow the instructions at Step 1: Create an Image Builder up to the **Network Access** section.

2. Choose **Default Internet Access**.

3. If **Subnet** is empty, select a subnet.

4. Continue with the instructions at Step 1: Create an Image Builder.

Enabling Internet Access Using a NAT Gateway

You can control internet access for your users using an advanced networking configuration such as NAT gateways. To manage your own VPC and VPC NAT gateway, launch your AppStream 2.0 image builders and fleets in private VPC subnets that provide a route to the internet. Use the instructions below to quickly create a network setup for enabling internet access. For more information, see NAT Gateways and VPC with Public and Private Subnets (NAT) in the *Amazon VPC User Guide*.

To create and configure a new VPC to use with a VPC NAT gateway

1. Navigate to Implementing VPC with Public and Private Subnets (NAT) in the *Amazon VPC User Guide*, and follow the steps given in the section **To create a VPC**, leaving out the optional IPv6 step.

2. For **Availability Zone**, leave the public subnet zone as the default, and select a specific zone for the private subnet. Make a note of the zones you chose.

3. For **Elastic IP Allocation ID**, choose an existing Elastic IP address. If you don't have one, create an Elastic IP address from the **Elastic IPs** section on the Amazon VPC console.

4. Leave the other fields as their default values, making a note of the value for **Private subnet's IPv4 CIDR**, and then choose **Create VPC**. This may take some time to complete.

5. If you want to add another private subnet to your VPC, perform the following steps.

    1. In the left navigation pane, choose **Subnets, Create Subnet**. Be sure to choose a different name than the ones specified in step 3.

    2. For **VPC**, enter the VPC that you created earlier. For **Availability Zone**, enter a different value than the one noted earlier.

    3. For **IPv4 CIDR block**, provide a unique for the new subnet. For example, if you noted that the first subnet has a IPv4 CIDR block range of 10.0.1.0/24, the new subnet could have a valid CIDR block range of 10.0.2.0/24.

6. Choose **Yes, Create**.

To add a NAT gateway to an existing VPC

1. Follow the instructions in Creating a NAT Gateway in the *Amazon VPC User Guide*.

2. To update the route tables of your private subnets and route internet traffic through the NAT gateway, follow the instructions in Updating Your Route Table in the *Amazon VPC User Guide*.

3. Check your VPC to be sure it has at least one private subnet and, if needed, create a new private subnet. For more information, see Creating a Subnet in the *Amazon VPC User Guide*.

Enabling Internet Access for a Fleet Using a NAT Gateway

After you have a NAT gateway available on a VPC, you can enable internet access for your fleet. This can be performed either when you create it, or by editing the fleet details after creation.

To enable internet access at fleet creation using a NAT gateway

1. Follow the instructions at Create a Fleet up to the **Network access** section.

2. Choose a VPC with a NAT gateway.

3. If the subnet fields are empty, select a private subnet for **Subnet 1** and, if desired, another private subnet for **Subnet 2**. If one is not already present for your VPC, you may need to create a second private subnet .

4. Continue with the instructions at Create a Fleet.

To enable internet access after fleet creation using a NAT gateway

1. In the navigation pane, choose **Fleets**.

2. Select a fleet and check that the state is **Stopped**.

3. Choose **Fleet Details**, **Edit**, and choose a VPC with a NAT gateway.

4. Choose a private subnet for **Subnet 1** and, if desired, another private **Subnet 2**. You may need to create a second private subnet if one is not already present for your VPC.

5. Choose **Update**.

You can test your internet connectivity by starting your fleet, and then connecting to your streaming instance and browsing to the internet.

Enabling Internet Access for an Image Builder Using a NAT Gateway

After you have a NAT gateway available on a VPC, and can enable internet access for your image builder. This can be performed when you create the image builder.

To enable internet access for an image builder using a NAT gateway

1. Follow the instructions at Step 1: Create an Image Builder, up to the **Network Access** section.

2. Choose the VPC with a NAT gateway.

3. If **Subnet** is empty, select a subnet.

4. Continue with the instructions at Step 1: Create an Image Builder.

AppStream 2.0 Image Builders

AppStream 2.0 provides virtual machines, or instances, that are used to install and add applications into and create your image. These instances are called *image builders*. You can launch an image builder from a base image provided by AWS, or from an image that you create. After your image builder instance is available (running), you can connect to the image builder to start a desktop session, install your applications, add your applications to an image, and create an image.

While launching a new image builder, you can choose from different instance types with various compute, memory, and graphics configurations. Note that the instance type must align with the instance family you need. For more information, see AppStream 2.0 Instance Families.

You also provide a VPC subnet so that AppStream 2.0 can establish a network interface to the image builder. This connection provides your image builder with access to resources that might be needed while you install and add applications; for example, file servers, licensing servers, database servers, and so on. For more information, see Tutorial: Create a Custom Image.

Actions

The following actions can be performed on an image builder, depending on the current state (status) of the image builder instance.

Delete
Permanently delete an image builder.
The instance must be in a **Stopped** state.

Connect
Connect to a running image builder. This action starts a desktop streaming session with the image builder to install and add applications to the image, and create an image.
The instance must be in a **Running** state.

Start
Start a stopped image builder. A running instance is billed to your account.
The instance must be in a **Stopped** state.

Stop
Stop a running image builder. A stopped instance is not billed to your account.
The instance must be in a **Running** state.

None of these actions can be performed on an instance in any of the following intermediate states:

- **Pending**
- **Snapshotting**
- **Stopping**
- **Starting**
- **Deleting**

Tutorial: Create a Custom Image

Before you can stream your applications, Amazon AppStream 2.0 requires at least one image that you create by using an image builder. This tutorial describes how to create custom images by using an image builder.

Important
After you create an image builder and it is running, your account may incur nominal charges. For more information, see AppStream 2.0 Pricing.

Important
This tutorial contains details that apply to the latest base image release. For more information, see Amazon AppStream 2.0 Windows Image Version History.
If you are using images that are created from base images dated before 2017-07-24, you can view a compatible version of this tutorial by downloading the PDF file appstream2-dg-2017-07-23.pdf.

Topics

- Step 1: Create an Image Builder
- Step 2: Install Applications on the Image Builder
- Step 3: Create an AppStream 2.0 Application Catalog
- Step 4: Create Default Application and Windows Settings
- Step 5: Test Applications
- Step 6: Optimize Applications
- Step 7: Finish Creating Your Image
- Step 8 (Optional): Tag and Copy an Image
- Step 9: Clean Up

Step 1: Create an Image Builder

In this step, create a new image builder so that you can add applications and create images for streaming.

To create an image builder for adding applications

1. Open the AppStream 2.0 console at https://console.aws.amazon.com/appstream2.

2. You can launch the image builder in the following ways:

    - If a welcome screen appears displaying two options (**Try it now** and **Get started**), choose **Get started, Custom set up**.

      For information about these two options, see Amazon AppStream 2.0 FAQs.

    - If a welcome screen does not appear, choose **Quick links** in the left navigation pane, then **Custom set up**.

    - Alternatively, choose **Images** in the left navigation pane, then the **Image Builder** tab, **Launch Image Builder**.

3. For **Step 1: Choose Image**, choose a base image. If you are launching the image builder for the first time, you can use one of the latest base images released by AWS (selected by default). For a list of the latest versions of base images released by AWS, see Amazon AppStream 2.0 Windows Image Version History. If you have already created images, or you want to update applications in an existing image, you can select one of your existing images. Be sure to select an image that aligns with the instance family that you need. For more information, see AppStream 2.0 Instance Families.

    Choose **Next**.

4. For **Step 2: Configure Image Builder**, configure the image builder by accepting the default values or providing inputs for the following fields:
    Name

Type a unique name identifier for the image builder.

Instance Type

Select the instance type for the image builder. Choose a type that matches the performance requirements of the applications that you plan to install. For more information, see AppStream 2.0 Instance Families. The AppStream 2.0 agent software runs on your streaming instances, enabling your users to connect to and stream their applications. Starting December 7, 2017, your streaming instances can be automatically updated with the latest AppStream 2.0 agent software. This capability helps to ensure that your image builder includes the latest features, performance improvements, and security updates that are available from AWS.

You can enable automatic updates of the AppStream 2.0 agent by creating a new image from any base image published by AWS on or after December 7, 2017. If the image from which you are launching your image builder is not using the latest version of the AppStream 2.0 agent, we recommend that you select the option to launch your image builder with the latest agent. This option is not displayed if you are already using the latest base image from AWS or if you are using a custom image that uses the latest version of the agent.

Choose **Next**.

5. Do the following:

   - For **Step 3: Configure Network**, choose a virtual private cloud (VPC) subnet in which to launch your image builder. Your image builder has access to any of the network resources that are accessible from within this VPC subnet.
   - For internet access on the image builder, choose **Default Internet Access**, select a VPC that has public subnets on your default VPC, and then select one of the public subnets listed for **Subnet**. If you are controlling internet access using a NAT gateway, leave **Default Internet Access** unselected and use the VPC with the NAT gateway. For more information, see Network Settings for Amazon AppStream 2.0 .
   - For **Security group(s)**, select up to five security groups to associate with this image builder. If needed, choose **Create new security group**. If you do not choose a security group, the image builder is associated with the default security group for your VPC. For more information, see Security Groups.
   - For **Active Directory Domain (Optional)**, expand this section to choose which Active Directory and organizational unit in which to place your streaming instance computer objects. Ensure that the selected network access settings enable DNS resolvability and communication with your directory. For more information, see Using Active Directory with AppStream 2.0.

6. Choose **Review** and confirm the details for the image builder. To change the configuration for any section, choose **Edit** and make the needed changes. After you finish reviewing the configuration details, choose **Launch**.

After the service prepares the needed resources, the image builder instance list appears. The status of your new image builder appears as **Running** when the image builder is ready to use.

Optionally, you can apply one or more tags to help manage the image builder. Choose **Tags**, choose **Add/Edit Tags**, choose **Add Tag**, specify the key and value for the tag, and then choose **Save**. For more information, see Tagging Your Amazon AppStream 2.0 Resources.

Step 2: Install Applications on the Image Builder

In this step, connect to the image builder that you created and launched, then install your applications on the image builder.

Important

To complete this step, you must log into the image builder with the local **Administrator** account or a domain user account that has local administrator permissions.

To install applications on the image builder

1. In the left navigation pane, choose **Images, Image Builder**.

2. Choose the image builder to use, verify that it is in the **Running** state, and choose **Connect**. For this step to work, you may need to configure your browser to allow pop-ups from https://stream/.<aws-region>.amazonappstream.com/.

3. Log in to the image builder by doing either of the following:

   - If your image builder is not joined to an Active Directory domain, on the **Local User** tab, choose **Administrator**.
   - If your image builder is joined to an Active Directory domain and you require access to resources that are managed by Active Directory to install your applications, choose the **Directory User** tab, type the credentials for a domain user account that has local administrator permissions on the image builder, then choose **Log in**.

4. Install applications from an application website or other download source. Install the applications you want before proceeding to the next step. **Note**
   Download and install applications only from sites that you trust.

   If an application requires the Windows operating system restart, let it do so. Before the operating system restarts, you are disconnected from your image builder. After the restart is complete, connect to the image builder again, then finish installing the application.

Step 3: Create an AppStream 2.0 Application Catalog

In this step, create an AppStream 2.0 application catalog by specifying applications (*.exe*), batch scripts (*.bat*), and application shortcuts (*.lnk*) for your image. For each application that you plan to stream, you can specify the name, display name, executable file to launch, and icon to display. If you choose an application shortcut, these values are prepopulated for you.

Important
To complete this step, you must be logged into the image builder with the local **Administrator** account or a domain user account that has local administrator permissions.

To create an AppStream 2.0 application catalog

1. From the image builder desktop, open Image Assistant. Image Assistant guides you through the image creation process.

2. In **1. Add Apps**, choose **+ Add App**, and navigate to the location of the application, script, or shortcut to add. Choose **Open**.

3. In the **App Launch Settings** dialog box, keep or change the default settings for **Name**, **Display Name**, and **Icon Path**. Optionally, you can specify launch parameters (additional arguments passed to the application when it is launched) and a working directory for the application. When you're done, choose **Save**.

   The **Display Name** and **Icon Path** settings determine how your application name and icon appear in the application catalog. The catalog displays to users when they sign in to an AppStream 2.0 streaming session.

4. Repeat steps 2 and 3 for each application in Image Assistant and confirm that the applications appear on the **Add Apps** tab. When you're done, choose **Next** to continue using Image Assistant to create your image.

Step 4: Create Default Application and Windows Settings

In this step, you create default application and Windows settings for your AppStream 2.0 users. Doing this enables your users to get started with applications quickly during their AppStream 2.0 streaming sessions, without the need to create or configure these settings themselves. For example, you can create and configure:

- Application preferences, including a browser home page, toolbar customizations, and security settings.
- Application data settings, including browser bookmarks and connection profiles.
- Windows experience settings, including displaying file name extensions and hidden folders.

Additionally, you can modify or disable Internet Explorer security settings such as Enhanced Security Configuration (ESC). For more information, see Disable Internet Explorer Enhanced Security Configuration.

Important
To complete this step, you must be logged into the image builder with the local **Template User** account or a domain user account that does not have local administrator permissions.

To create default application and Windows settings for your users

1. In Image Assistant, in **2. Configure Apps**, choose **Switch user**. This disconnects you from the current session and displays the login menu.

2. Do either of the following:

   - If your image builder is not joined to an Active Directory domain, on the **Local User** tab, choose **Template User**. This account enables you to create your default application and Windows settings.
   - If your image builder is joined to an Active Directory domain, choose **Directory User**, and log in as a domain user that does not have local administrator permissions.

3. From the image builder desktop, open Image Assistant, which displays the applications that you added when you created the application catalog.

4. Choose the application for which you want to create default application settings.

5. After the application opens, create these settings as needed.

6. When you're done, close the application, and return to Image Assistant.

7. If you specified more than one application in Image Assistant, repeat steps 4 through 6 for each application as needed.

8. If you want default Windows settings, create them now. When you're done, return to Image Assistant.

9. Choose **Switch user** and log in with the same account that you used to create the application catalog (an account that has local administrator permissions).

10. In Image Assistant, in **2. Configure Apps**, do either of the following:

    - If your image builder is not joined to an Active Directory domain, choose **Save settings**.

    - If your image builder is joined to an Active Directory domain, in the **Choose which user settings to copy **list, choose the same account that you used to log into the image builder when you created the default application and Windows settings, then choose **Save settings**.

      The **Choose which settings to copy** list displays any user account that currently has settings saved on the image builder.

11. When you're done, choose **Next** to continue creating your image.

Step 5: Test Applications

In this step, verify that the applications you've added open correctly and perform as expected. To do so, start a new Windows session as a user who has the same permissions as your users.

Important
To complete this step, you must log in to the image builder with the **Test User** account or a domain user account that does not have local administrator permissions.

To test your applications

1. In Image Assistant, in **3. Test**, do either of the following:

   - If your image builder is not joined to an Active Directory domain, choose **Switch user**.
   - If your image builder is joined to an Active Directory domain, you require a domain user account to test your applications, and the user already has settings on the image builder, you must reset the application settings for that user. To do so, select the user from the **User to reset** list, and choose **Reset**. When you're done, choose **Switch user. Note**
     If your image builder is new and no users have settings on the image builder, the list does not display any users.

2. Choose the user account to use for testing by doing either of the following:

   - If your image builder is not joined to an Active Directory domain, choose **Test User**. This account enables you to test your applications by using the same policies and permissions as your users.
   - If your image builder is joined to an Active Directory domain, choose **Directory User**, specify the credentials for a domain user account that does not have local administrator permissions, then choose **Log in**.

3. From the image builder desktop, open Image Assistant, which displays the applications that you specified when you created the application catalog.

4. Choose the application that you want to test, to confirm that it opens correctly and that any default application settings you created are applied.

5. After the application opens, test it as needed. When you're done, close the application and return to Image Assistant.

6. If you specified more than one application in Image Assistant, repeat steps 4 and 5 to test each application as needed.

7. When you're done, choose **Switch user**, then do either of the following:

   - If your image builder is not joined to an Active Directory domain, on the **Local User** tab, choose **Administrator**.
   - If your image builder is joined to an Active Directory domain and you logged in as a domain user with local administrator permissions to specify applications in Image Assistant, log in as that user.

8. Choose **Next** to continue creating your image.

Step 6: Optimize Applications

In this step, Image Assistant opens your applications one after another, identifies their launch dependencies, and performs optimizations to ensure that applications launch quickly. These are required steps that are performed on all applications in the list.

To optimize your applications

1. In Image Assistant, in **4. Optimize**, choose **Launch**.

2. AppStream 2.0 automatically launches the first application in your list. When the application completely starts, provide any required input to perform the first run experience for the application. For example, a web browser may prompt you to import settings before it is completely up and running.

3. After you complete the first run experience and verify that the application performs as expected, choose **Continue**. If you added more than one application to your image, each application opens automatically. Repeat this step for each application as needed, leaving all applications running.

4. When you're done, the next tab in Image Assistant, **5. Configure Image**, automatically displays.

Step 7: Finish Creating Your Image

In this step, choose an image name and finish creating your image.

To create the image

1. Type a unique image name, an image display name, a description if you want, and choose **Next**. The name you choose cannot begin with "Amazon," "AWS," or "AppStream." When you're done, choose **Next**.
   Note
   If you choose a base image that is published by AWS on or after December 7, 2017, the option **Always use the latest agent version** appears, selected by default. We recommend that you leave this option selected so that streaming instances that are launched from the image always use the latest version of the agent. If you disable this option, you cannot enable it after you finish creating the image. For information about the latest release of the AppStream 2.0 agent, see Amazon AppStream 2.0 Agent Version History.

2. In **6. Review**, verify the image details. To make changes, choose **Previous** to navigate to the appropriate Image Assistant tab, make your changes, and then proceed through the steps in Image Assistant as needed.

3. After you finish reviewing the image details, choose **Disconnect and Create Image**.

4. The remote session disconnects within a few moments. When the **Lost Connectivity** message appears, close the browser tab. While the image is created, the image builder status appears as **Snapshotting**. You cannot connect to the image builder until this process finishes.

5. Return to the console and navigate to **Images, Image Registry**. Verify that your new image appears in the list.

   While your image is being created, the image status in the image registry of the console appears as **Pending** and you cannot connect to it.

6. Choose the **Refresh** icon periodically to update the status. After your image is created, the image status changes to **Available** and the image builder is automatically stopped.

   To continue creating images, start the image builder and connect to it from the console, or create a new image builder.

Note
To change your image, such as add other applications or update existing applications, you must create a new image. To do so, restart and reconnect to the image builder, make your changes, and then repeat the Image Assistant process to create a new image that includes the changes.

Step 8 (Optional): Tag and Copy an Image

After you create an image, you can apply one or more tags to help manage the image. You can also copy the image within the same region or to a new region within the same AWS account. Copying a source image results in an identical but distinct destination image. AWS does not copy any user-defined tags, however. Also, you can only copy custom images that you create, not the base images that are provided by AWS.

Note
You can copy up to two images at the same time to a destination. If the destination to which you are copying an image is at the image limit, you receive an error. To copy the image in this case, you must first remove images from the destination. After the destination is below the image limit, initiate the image copy from the source region. For more information, see Amazon AppStream 2.0 Service Limits.

To add tags to an image

1. In the navigation pane, choose **Images, Image Registry**.

2. In the image list, select the image to which you want to add tags.

3. Choose **Tags**, choose **Add/Edit Tags**, choose **Add Tag**, specify the key and value for the tag, and then choose **Save**.

For more information, see Tagging Your Amazon AppStream 2.0 Resources.

To copy an image

Copying an image across geographically diverse regions enables you to stream applications from multiple regions based on the same image. By streaming your applications in closer proximity to your users, you can improve your users' experience streaming applications with AppStream 2.0.

1. In the navigation pane, choose **Images**, **Image Registry**.

2. In the image list, select the image that you want to copy.

3. Choose **Actions**, **Copy**.

4. In the **Copy Image** dialog box, specify the following information, and then choose **Copy Image:**

   - For **Destination region**, choose the region to which to copy the new image.
   - For **Name**, specify a name that the image will have when it is copied to the destination.
   - For **Description** (optional), specify a description that the image will have when it is copied to the destination.

5. To check on the progress of the copy operation, return to the console and navigate to **Images**, **Image Registry**. Use the navigation bar to switch to the destination region (if applicable), and confirm that your new image appears in the list of images.

   The new image first appears with a status of **Copying** in the image registry of your console. After the image is successfully created, the status of the image changes to **Available**, which means that you can use the image to launch a stack and stream your applications.

Step 9: Clean Up

Finally, stop your running image builders to free up resources and avoid unintended charges to your account. We recommend stopping any unused, running image builders. For more information, see AppStream 2.0 Pricing.

To stop a running image builder

1. In the navigation pane, choose **Images**, **Image Builders**, and select the running image builder instance.

2. Choose **Actions**, **Stop**.

AppStream 2.0 Images

An Amazon AppStream 2.0 image contains applications that can be streamed to users. The image is used to launch streaming instances that are part of an AppStream 2.0 fleet. All images available to you are listed under the **Image Registry** section in the AWS Management Console. Note that the image's instance family must align with the instance type you need. For more information, see AppStream 2.0 Instance Families.

The images in your image registry are differentiated by these visibility attributes:

- **Public Images** — Base images that are made available by AWS to help you create images with your own applications.
- **Private Images** — Images that are created and owned by you.

You can use either public or private images to launch an image builder and set up your AppStream 2.0 fleet. For more information, see Tutorial: Create a Custom Image.

You can also delete your private images. Note that a private image cannot be deleted if there are active fleets using it. You must stop all associated fleets before deleting the image.

Amazon AppStream 2.0 Windows Image Version History

AWS publishes base images to help you create images that include your own applications. Base images include the latest Windows operating system and the AppStream 2.0 agent software. For information about the latest AppStream 2.0 software, see Amazon AppStream 2.0 Agent Version History.

The following are the latest images:

- **Base** — Base-Image-Builder-06-12-2018
- **Graphics Design** — Graphics-Design-Image-Builder-06-12-2018
- **Graphics Desktop** — Graphics-Desktop-Image-Builder-06-12-2018
- **Graphics Pro** — Graphics-Pro-Image-Builder-06-12-2018

The latest base image released on June 12, 2018 includes the following software components:

- **Amazon SSM Agent** — 2.2.619.0
- **Amazon WDDM Hook Driver** — 1.0.0.56
- **EC2Config service** — 4.9.2644

The following table describes all released images.

Release	Image	Description
06-12-2018	[See the AWS documentation website for more details]	[See the AWS documentation website for more details]
05-02-2018	[See the AWS documentation website for more details]	[See the AWS documentation website for more details]
03-19-2018	[See the AWS documentation website for more details]	[See the AWS documentation website for more details]
01-24-2018	[See the AWS documentation website for more details]	[See the AWS documentation website for more details]
01-01-2018	[See the AWS documentation website for more details]	[See the AWS documentation website for more details]
12-07-2017	[See the AWS documentation website for more details]	[See the AWS documentation website for more details]
11-13-2017	[See the AWS documentation website for more details]	[See the AWS documentation website for more details]
09-05-2017	[See the AWS documentation website for more details]	[See the AWS documentation website for more details]
07-25-2017	[See the AWS documentation website for more details]	[See the AWS documentation website for more details]
07-24-2017	[See the AWS documentation website for more details]	[See the AWS documentation website for more details]
06-20-2017	[See the AWS documentation website for more details]	[See the AWS documentation website for more details]
05-18-2017	[See the AWS documentation website for more details]	[See the AWS documentation website for more details]

Amazon AppStream 2.0 Agent Version History

The Amazon AppStream 2.0 agent software runs on your streaming instances, enabling end users to connect to and start their streaming applications. Starting December 7, 2017, your streaming instances can be automatically updated with the latest features, performance improvements, and security updates that are available from AWS. Before December 7, 2017, agent updates were included with new base image releases.

To use the latest AppStream 2.0 agent software, you need to rebuild your images by using new base images published by AWS on or after December 7, 2017. When you do this, the option to enable automatic updates of the agent is selected by default in the Image Assistant. We recommend that you leave this option selected so that any new image builder or fleet instance that is launched from your image always uses the latest version of the agent. For more information, see Tutorial: Create a Custom Image.

The following table describes the latest updates that are available in released versions of the AppStream 2.0 agent.

Amazon AppStream 2.0 agent version	Description
06-06-2018	[See the AWS documentation website for more details]
05-31-2018	[See the AWS documentation website for more details]
05-21-2018	[See the AWS documentation website for more details]
03-19-2018	[See the AWS documentation website for more details]
01-24-2018	[See the AWS documentation website for more details]
12-07-2017	[See the AWS documentation website for more details]

Amazon AppStream 2.0 Fleets and Stacks

With Amazon AppStream 2.0, you create stacks and fleets as part of the process of streaming applications. A fleet consists of streaming instances that run the image that you specify. A stack consists of an associated fleet, user access policies, and storage configurations.

Topics

- Fleet Type
- Session Context
- Instance Families
- Create Fleets and Stacks
- Customize Fleets
- Fleet Auto Scaling

Fleet Type

The fleet type determines when your instances run and how you pay for them. You can specify a fleet type when you create a fleet. You cannot change the fleet type after you create the fleet.

The following are the possible fleet types:

Always-On
Instances run all the time, even when no users are streaming applications.

On-Demand
Instances run only when users are streaming applications. Idle instances that are available for streaming are in a stopped state.

Use an Always-On fleet to provide your users with instant access to their applications. Use an On-Demand fleet to optimize your streaming charges and provide your users with access to their applications after a 1-2 minute wait. For more information, see Amazon AppStream 2.0 Pricing.

To create an On-Demand fleet, you must use a base image starting with 09-05-2017.

Session Context

You can pass parameters to your streaming application using *session context*. The format is a string with parameters separated by commas. Session context is supported using the AWS CLI and the AWS SDKs, but is not supported using the AWS Management Console.

Starting with the images released on 09-05-2017, the parameters are passed using the `AppStream_Session_Context` environment variable. This environment variable is accessible only through .NET, and we provide an executable file, `SessionContextRetriever.exe`, that you can use to access it. With images released prior to 09-05-2017, parameters are passed to the application.

The following example uses session context to launch a specific website using Google Chrome.

To use session context to launch a website

1. Connect to your image builder in Administrator mode. For this example, install Google Chrome on the image builder.

2. Create a child folder of `C:\`. For this example, use `C:\Scripts`.

3. For images released on or after 09-05-2017, download SessionContextRetriever.exe.

4. Create a Windows batch file in the new folder. For this example, create `C:\Scripts\session-context-test.bat` and add a script that launches Chrome with the URL from session context, and then waits for keyboard input.

For images released on or after 09-05-2017, use the following script:

```
1 for /f "tokens=* USEBACKQ" %%f in (`SessionContextRetriever.exe`) do (
2 set var=%%f
3 )
4 chrome.exe %var%
5 pause
```

For images released prior to 09-05-2017, use the following scripts:

```
1 chrome.exe %1
2 pause
```

5. In Image Assistant, add `session-context-test.bat` and change the working directory to `C:\Program Files (x86)\Google\Chrome\Application`.

6. Create an image, fleet, and stack. For this example, use a fleet name of **session-context-test-fleet** and a stack name of **session-context-test-stack**.

7. After the fleet is running, you can call create-streaming-url with the **session-context** parameter, as shown in this example.

```
1 aws appstream create-streaming-url --stack-name session-context-test-stack \
2 --fleet-name session-context-test-fleet \
3 --user-id username -validity 10000 \
4 --application-id chrome --session-context "www.google.com"
```

8. Open the streaming URL in a browser. The batch file launches Chrome and loads `http://www.google.com`.

AppStream 2.0 Instance Families

Amazon AppStream 2.0 users stream applications from stacks created by an administrator. Each stack is associated with a fleet. When you create a fleet, the instance type that you specify determines the hardware of the host computers used for your fleet. Each instance type offers different compute, memory, and GPU capabilities. Instance types are grouped into *instance families* based on these capabilities.

When you create a fleet or image builder, you must select an image that is compatible with the instance family on which you intend to run your fleet.

- When launching a new image builder, you are presented with a list of the images in your image registry. Select the appropriate base image.
- When launching a fleet, ensure that the private image you select was created from the appropriate base image.

The following table summarizes the available instance families and provides the base image naming format for each. Select an instance type from an instance family based on the requirements of the applications that you plan to stream on your fleet, and match the base image according to the following table.

Instance Family	Description	Base Image Name
General Purpose	Basic computing resources for running web browsers and most business applications.	Base-Image-Builder-MM-DD-YYYY
Memory Optimized	Optimized for memory-intensive applications that process large amounts of data.	Base-Image-Builder-MM-DD-YYYY
Compute Optimized	Optimized for compute-bound applications that benefit from high performance processors.	Base-Image-Builder-MM-DD-YYYY
Graphics Design	Uses AMD FirePro S7150x2 Server GPUs and AMD Multiuser GPU technology to support graphics applications that use DirectX, OpenGL, or OpenCL.	Graphics-Design-Image-Builder-MM-DD-YYYY
Graphics Desktop	Uses NVIDIA GRID K520 GPU to support applications that benefit from or require graphics acceleration. This instance family supports DirectX, OpenGL, OpenCL, and CUDA.	Graphics-Desktop-Image-Builder-MM-DD-YYYY
Graphics Pro	Uses NVIDIA Tesla M60 GPUs and provide a high-performance, workstation-like experience for graphics applications that use DirectX, OpenGL, OpenCL, or CUDA.	Graphics-Pro-Image-Builder-MM-DD-YYYY

For more information, see the following:

- Amazon AppStream 2.0 Windows Image Version History
- Amazon AppStream 2.0 Service Limits
- AppStream 2.0 Pricing

Create AppStream 2.0 Fleets and Stacks

To stream your applications, Amazon AppStream 2.0 requires an environment that includes a fleet that is associated with a stack, and at least one application image. This tutorial describes the steps to set up a fleet and stack, and how to give users access to the stack. If you haven't already done so, we recommend that you try the procedures in Getting Started with Amazon AppStream 2.0 first.

If you want to create an image to use, see Tutorial: Create a Custom Image.

If you plan to join a fleet to an Active Directory domain, configure your Active Directory domain before completing the following steps. For more information, see Using Active Directory with AppStream 2.0.

Topics

- Create a Fleet
- Create a Stack
- Provide Access to Users
- Clean Up Resources

Create a Fleet

Set up and create a fleet from which user applications are launched and streamed.

To set up and create a fleet

1. Open the AppStream 2.0 console at https://console.aws.amazon.com/appstream2.

2. Choose **Get Started** if you are new to the console, or **Fleets** from the left navigation pane. Choose **Create Fleet**.

3. For **Step 1: Provide Fleet Details**, provide a fleet name, optional display name, and optional description. Choose **Next**.

4. For **Step 2: Choose an Image**, choose an image that meets your needs and then choose **Next**.

5. For **Step 3: Configure Fleet**, do the following:

   1. For **Choose instance type**, choose the instance type that meets the performance requirements of your applications.

   2. For **Fleet type**, choose the fleet type that suits your use case. The fleet type determines its immediate availability and how you pay for it.

   3. For **Maximum session duration** — Choose the maximum amount of time that a streaming session can remain active. If users are still connected to a streaming session five minutes before this limit is reached, they are prompted to save any open documents before being disconnected.

   4. For **Disconnect timeout**, choose the time that a streaming instance should remain active after users disconnect. If users try to reconnect to the streaming session after a disconnection or network interruption within this time interval, they are connected to the previous session. Otherwise, they are connected to a new session with a new instance. If you associate a stack with a fleet for which a redirect URL is specified, after users' streaming sessions end, the users are redirected to that URL.

      If a user ends the session by choosing **End Session** on the streaming session toolbar, the disconnect timeout does not apply. Instead, the user is prompted to save any open documents, and then immediately disconnected from the streaming instance.

   5. For **Minimum capacity**, choose a minimum number of instances for your fleet based on the minimum number of expected concurrent users.

6. For **Maximum capacity**, choose a maximum number of instances for your fleet based on the maximum number of expected concurrent users.

7. For **Scaling details**, specify the scaling policies that AppStream 2.0 uses to increase and decrease the capacity of your fleet. Note that the size of your fleet is limited by the minimum and maximum capacity that you specified. For more information, see Fleet Auto Scaling for Amazon AppStream 2.0.

6. For **Step 4: Configure Network**, do the following:

   1. To add internet access for fleet instances in a VPC with a public subnet, choose **Default Internet Access**. If you are providing internet access using a NAT gateway, leave **Default Internet Access** unselected. For more information, see Network Settings for Amazon AppStream 2.0 .

   2. Choose a VPC and two subnets with access to the network resources that your application needs. If you don't have a VPC or subnets, you can create them using the links provided and then click the refresh icons.

   3. For **Security groups**, select up to five security groups to associate with this fleet. Otherwise, the default security group for the VPC is used. If you need to create a security group, use the link provided and then click the refresh icon.

   4. For **Active Directory Domain (Optional)**, choose the Active Directory and organizational unit (OU) for your streaming instance computer objects. Ensure that the network access settings you selected enable DNS resolvability and communication with your directory. For more information, see Using Active Directory with AppStream 2.0.

7. Choose **Create**.

   While your fleet is being created and fleet instances are provisioned, the status of your fleets displays as **Starting** in the **Fleets** list. Choose the **Refresh** icon periodically to update the fleet status until the status is **Running**. You cannot associate the fleet with a stack and use it for streaming sessions until the status of the fleet is **Running**.

   Optionally, you can apply one or more tags to help manage the fleet. Choose **Tags**, choose **Add/Edit Tags**, choose **Add Tag**, specify the key and value for the tag, and then choose **Save**. For more information, see Tagging Your Amazon AppStream 2.0 Resources.

Create a Stack

Set up and create a stack to control access to your fleet.

To set up and create a stack

1. In the left navigation pane, choose **Stacks**, and then choose **Create Stack**.

2. For **Step 1: Stack Details**, provide a stack name. Optionally, you can provide the following:

   - **Display name** — Enter a name to display for the stack (maximum of 100 characters).
   - **Description**— Enter a description for the stack (maximum of 256 characters).
   - **Redirect URL** — Specify a URL to which users are redirected after their streaming sessions end.
   - **Feedback URL** — Specify a URL to which users are redirected after they click the **Send Feedback** link to submit feedback about their application streaming experience. If you do not specify a URL, this link is not displayed.
   - **Fleet** — Select an existing fleet or create a new one to associate with your stack.

3. Choose **Next.**

4. For **Step 2: Enable Storage**, you can provide persistent storage for your users by choosing either or both of the following:

- **Enable Home Folders** — Users can save their files to their home folder and access existing files in their home folder during application streaming sessions. For information about requirements for enabling home folders, see Enable Home Folders for Your AppStream 2.0 Users.
- **Enable Google Drive** — Users can link their Google Drive account to AppStream 2.0, and during application streaming sessions, they can sign in to their Google Drive account, save files to Google Drive, and access their existing files in Google Drive. You can enable Google Drive for accounts in G Suite domains only, not for personal Gmail accounts. **Note**
  After you select **Enable Google Drive**, type at least one G Suite domain name. Access to Google Drive during application streaming sessions will be limited to user accounts that are in the domains that you specify. You can specify up to 10 G Suite domains. For more information about requirements for enabling Google Drive, see Enable Google Drive for Your AppStream 2.0 Users.

5. Choose **Next**.

6. For **Step 3: User Settings**, select the ways in which your users can transfer data between their streaming session and their local device. When you're done, choose **Review**:

- **Clipboard** — By default, users can copy and paste data between their local device and streaming applications. You can limit Clipboard options so that users can paste data to their remote streaming session only or copy data to their local device only, or you can disable Clipboard options entirely. Note that users can still copy and paste between applications in their streaming session.
- **File transfer** — By default, users can upload and download files between their local device and streaming session. You can limit file transfer options so that users can upload files to their streaming session only or download files to their local device only, or you can disable file transfer entirely.
- **Print to local device** — By default, users can print to their local device from within a streaming application. When they choose **Print** in the application, they can download a .pdf file that they can print to a local printer. You can disable this option to prevent users from printing to a local device. **Note**
  These settings affect only whether users can use AppStream 2.0 data transfer features. If your image provides access to a browser, network printer, or other remote resource, your users might be able to transfer data to or from their streaming session in other ways.

7. For **Step 4: Review**, confirm the details for the stack. To change the configuration for any section, choose **Edit **and make the needed changes. After you finish reviewing the configuration details, choose **Create**.

After the service sets up resources, the **Stacks** page appears. The status of your new stack appears as **Active** when it is ready to use.

Optionally, you can apply one or more tags to help manage the stack. Choose **Tags**, choose **Add/Edit Tags**, choose **Add Tag**, specify the key and value for the tag, and then choose **Save**. For more information, see Tagging Your Amazon AppStream 2.0 Resources.

Provide Access to Users

After you create a stack with an associated fleet, you can provide access to users through the AppStream 2.0 user pool. For more information, see User Pool Administration.

Note that user pool users cannot be assigned to stacks with fleets that are joined to an Active Directory domain.

Clean Up Resources

You can stop your running fleet and delete your active stack to free up resources and to avoid unintended charges to your account. We recommend stopping any unused, running fleets.

Note that you cannot delete a stack with an associated fleet.

To clean up your resources

1. In the navigation pane, choose **Stacks**.

2. Select the stack and choose **Actions, Disassociate Fleet**.

3. From **Stack Details**, open the **Associated Fleet** link to select the fleet.

4. Choose **Actions, Stop**. It takes about 5 minutes to stop a fleet.

5. When the status of the fleet is **Stopped**, choose **Actions, Delete**.

6. In the navigation pane, choose **Stacks**.

7. Select the stack and choose **Actions, Delete**.

Customize AppStream 2.0 Fleets

By customizing AppStream 2.0 fleet instances, you can define specific aspects of your AppStream 2.0 environment to optimize your users' application streaming experience. For example, you can persist environment variables to dynamically pass settings across applications and set default file associations that are applied to all of your users. At a high level, customizing a fleet instance includes the following tasks:

- Connecting to an image builder and customizing it as needed.
- On the image builder, using Image Assistant to create a new image that includes your customizations.
- Creating a new fleet instance or modifying an existing one. When you configure the fleet instance, select the new customized image that you created.
- Creating a new stack or modifying an existing one and associating it with your fleet instance.

Note

For certain fleet customizations, in Active Directory environments, you might need to use the Group Policy Management Console (GPMC) to update Group Policy object (GPO) settings on a domain-joined computer.

Topics

- Persist Environment Variables
- Set Default File Associations for Your Users
- Set Google Chrome as the Default Browser for Users' Streaming Sessions
- Disable Internet Explorer Enhanced Security Configuration
- Change the Default Internet Explorer Home Page for Users' Streaming Sessions

Persist Environment Variables

Environment variables enable you to dynamically pass settings across applications. For example, many engineering applications rely on environment variables to specify the IP address or host name of a license server to locate and check out a license from that server.

Follow the steps in these procedures to make environment variables available across your fleet instances.

Topics

- Change System Environment Variables
- Change User Environment Variables
- Create an Environment Variable That is Limited in Scope

Note

If you are using Active Directory and Group Policy with AppStream 2.0, keep in mind that streaming instances must be joined to an Active Directory domain to use Group Policy for environment variables. For information about how to configure the Group Policy **Environment Variable** preference item, see Configure an Environment Variable Item in the Microsoft documentation.

Change System Environment Variables

Follow these steps to change system environment variables across your fleet instances.

To change system environment variables on an image builder

This procedure applies only to system environment variables, not user environment variables. To change user environment variables that persist across your fleet instances, follow the steps in the next procedure.

1. Open the AppStream 2.0 console at https://console.aws.amazon.com/appstream2.

2. In the left navigation pane, choose **Images**, **Image Builder**.

3. Choose the image builder on which to change system environment variables, verify that it is in the **Running** state, and choose **Connect**.

4. Log in to the image builder by doing either of the following:

   - If your image builder is not joined to an Active Directory domain, on the **Local User** tab, choose **Administrator**.
   - If your image builder is joined to an Active Directory domain, choose the **Directory User** tab, specify the credentials for a domain user account that has local administrator permissions on the image builder, then choose **Log in**.

5. Choose the Windows **Start** button, open the context (right-click) menu for **Computer**, and then choose **Properties**.

6. In the navigation pane, choose **Advanced system settings**.

7. In **System variables**, change the environment variables that you want to persist across your fleet instances, and then choose** OK**.

8. On the image builder desktop, open Image Assistant.

9. Follow the necessary steps in Image Assistant to finish creating your image. For more information, see Tutorial: Create a Custom Image.

   The changes to the system environment variables persist across your fleet instances and are available to streaming sessions launched from those instances. **Note**
   Setting AWS CLI credentials as system environment variables might prevent AppStream 2.0 from creating the image.

Change User Environment Variables

Follow these steps to change user environment variables across your fleet instances.

To change user environment variables

1. Open the AppStream 2.0 console at https://console.aws.amazon.com/appstream2.

2. In the left navigation pane, choose **Images**, **Image Builder**.

3. Choose the image builder on which to change user environment variables, verify that it is in the **Running** state, and choose **Connect**.

4. On the **Local User** tab, choose **Template User**.

5. On the image builder, choose the Windows **Start** button, **Control Panel**, **User Accounts**.

6. Choose **User Accounts** again. In the left navigation pane, choose **Change my environment variables.**

7. Under **User environment variables** for **DefaultProfileUser**, set or create the user environment variables as needed, then choose **OK**.

8. This disconnects your current session and opens the login menu. Log in to the image builder by doing either of the following:

   - If your image builder is not joined to an Active Directory domain, on the **Local User** tab, choose **Administrator**.
   - If your image builder is joined to an Active Directory domain, choose the **Directory User** tab, and log in as a domain user who has local administrator permissions on the image builder.

9. On the image builder desktop, open Image Assistant.

10. Follow the necessary steps in Image Assistant to finish creating your image. For more information, see Tutorial: Create a Custom Image.

Create an Environment Variable That is Limited in Scope

Follow these steps to create an environment variable that is limited in scope to the processes that are spawned off the script. This approach is useful when you need to use the same environment variable name with different values for different applications. For example, if you have two different applications that use the environment variable "LIC_SERVER", but each application has a different value for "LIC_SERVER".

To create an environment variable that is limited in scope

1. Open the AppStream 2.0 console at https://console.aws.amazon.com/appstream2.

2. In the left navigation pane, choose **Images**, **Image Builder**.

3. Choose the image builder on which to create an environment variable that is limited in scope, verify that it is in the **Running** state, and choose **Connect**.

4. Log in to the image builder by doing either of the following:

   - If your image builder is not joined to an Active Directory domain, on the **Local User** tab, choose **Administrator**.
   - If your image builder is joined to an Active Directory domain, choose the **Directory User** tab, specify the credentials for a domain user account that has local administrator permissions on the image builder, then choose **Log in**.

5. Create a child folder of C:\ drive for the script (for example, C:\Scripts).

6. Open Notepad to create the new script, and enter the following lines:

   set *variable=value*

   start " " "C:\path\to\application.exe"

   Where:

   variable is the variable name to be used

   value is the value for the given variable name **Note**
   If the application path includes spaces, the entire string must be encapsulated within quotation marks. For example:
   start " " "C:\Program Files\application.exe"

7. Choose** File**, **Save**. Name the file and save it with the .bat extension to C:\Scripts. For example, name the file LaunchApp.bat.

8. If needed, repeat steps 4 and 5 to create a script for each additional application that requires its own environment variable and values.

9. On the image builder desktop, start Image Assistant.

10. Choose **Add App**, navigate to C:\Scripts, and select one of the scripts that you created in step 5. Choose **Open**.

11. In the **App Launch Settings** dialog box, keep or change the settings as needed. When you're done, choose **Save**.

12. If you created multiple scripts, repeat steps 8 and 9 for each script.

13. Follow the necessary steps in Image Assistant to finish creating your image. For more information, see Tutorial: Create a Custom Image.

    The environment variable and specific value are now available for processes that are run from the script. Other processes cannot access this variable and value.

Set Default File Associations for Your Users

The associations for application file extensions are set on a per-user basis and so are not automatically applied to all users who launch AppStream 2.0 streaming sessions. For example, if you set Adobe Reader as the default application for .pdf files on your image builder, this change is not applied to your users.

To set default file associations for your users

1. Open the AppStream 2.0 console at https://console.aws.amazon.com/appstream2.

2. Choose the image builder on which to set default file associations, verify that it is in the **Running** state, and choose **Connect**.

3. Log in to the image builder by doing either of the following:

   - If your image builder is not joined to an Active Directory domain, on the **Local User** tab, choose **Administrator**.
   - If your image builder is joined to an Active Directory domain, choose the **Directory User** tab, specify the credentials for a domain user account that has local administrator permissions on the image builder, then choose **Log in**.

4. Set default file associations as needed.

5. Open the Windows command prompt as an administrator.

6. At the command prompt, type the following command to export the image builder file associations as an XML file, and then press ENTER:

   `dism.exe/online/export-DefaultAppAssociations:c:\default_associations.xml`

   If you receive an error message stating that you cannot service a running 64-bit operating system with a 32-bit version of DISM, close the command prompt window. Open File Explorer, browse to C:\Windows\System32, right-click cmd.exe, choose **Run as Administrator**, and run the command again.

7. Open Local Group Policy Editor by opening the command prompt as an administrator, typing `gpedit.msc`, and then pressing ENTER.

8. In the console tree, under **Computer Configuration**, expand **Administrative Templates**, **Windows Components**, and then choose **File Explorer**.

9. Double-click **Set a default associations configuration file**.

10. In the **Set a default associations configuration file properties** dialog box, choose **Enabled**, and enter this path: `c:\default_associations.xml`.

11. Choose **Apply**, **OK**.

12. Close Local Group Policy Editor.

13. On the image builder desktop, open Image Assistant.

14. Follow the necessary steps in Image Assistant to finish creating your image. For more information, see Tutorial: Create a Custom Image.

    The file associations that you configured are applied to the fleet instances and user streaming sessions that are launched from those instances.

Set Google Chrome as the Default Browser for Users' Streaming Sessions

By default, new user accounts for Microsoft Windows have Internet Explorer set as the default browser. Follow these steps to set Google Chrome as the default browser for your fleet instances.

To set Google Chrome as the default browser for fleet instances

1. Open the AppStream 2.0 console at https://console.aws.amazon.com/appstream2.

2. Choose the image builder on which to set Chrome as the default browser, verify that it is in the **Running** state, and choose **Connect**.

3. Log in to the image builder by doing either of the following:

   - If your image builder is not joined to an Active Directory domain, on the **Local User** tab, choose **Administrator**.
   - If your image builder is joined to an Active Directory domain, choose the **Directory User** tab, specify the credentials for a domain user account that has local administrator permissions on the image builder, then choose **Log in**.

4. On the image builder desktop, start Image Assistant.

5. Choose **+ Add App**, navigate to the location where Chrome is installed (for example, C:\Program Files (x86)\Google\Chrome\Application\), and select chrome.exe.

6. In the **App Launch Settings** dialog box, in **Launch Parameters**, enter the following:

   ```
   --make-default-browser-for-user --no-first-run
   ```

7. Choose **Save**.

8. Continue installing and configuring applications as needed.

   Users who are connected to streaming sessions launched from those fleet instances have Google Chrome as the default browser for http:// and https:// connections. The users' existing application preferences for opening files with .htm and .html extensions are not changed.

Disable Internet Explorer Enhanced Security Configuration

Internet Explorer Enhanced Security Configuration (ESC) places servers and Internet Explorer in a configuration that limits exposure to the internet. However, this configuration can impact the AppStream 2.0 end user experience. Users who are connected to AppStream 2.0 streaming sessions may find that websites do not display or perform as expected when:

- Internet Explorer ESC is enabled on fleet instances from which users' streaming sessions are launched
- Users run Internet Explorer during their streaming sessions
- Applications use Internet Explorer to load data

To disable Internet Explorer Enhanced Security Configuration

1. Open the AppStream 2.0 console at https://console.aws.amazon.com/appstream2.

2. In the left navigation pane, choose **Images**, **Image Builder**.

3. Choose the image builder on which to disable Internet Explorer ESC, verify that it is in the **Running** state, and choose **Connect**.

4. Log in to the image builder by doing either of the following:

   - If your image builder is not joined to an Active Directory domain, on the **Local User** tab, choose **Administrator**.
   - If your image builder is joined to an Active Directory domain, choose the **Directory User** tab, specify the credentials for a domain user account that has local administrator permissions on the image builder, then choose **Log in**.

5. On the image builder, disable Internet Explorer ESC by doing the following:

   1. Open Server Manager. Choose the Windows **Start** button, and then choose **Server Manager**.

   2. In the left navigation pane, choose **Local Server**.

47

3. In the right properties pane, choose the **On** link next to IE Enhanced Security Configuration****.

4. In the **Internet Explorer Enhanced Configuration** dialog box, choose the **Off** option under **Administrators** and **Users**, then choose **OK**.

6. In the upper right area of the image builder desktop, choose **Admin Commands**, **Switch User**.

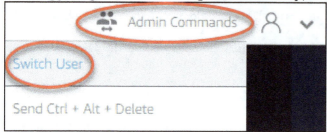

7. This disconnects your current session and opens the login menu. Log in to the image builder by doing either of the following:

   - If your image builder is not joined to an Active Directory domain, on the **Local User** tab, choose **Template User**.
   - If your image builder is joined to an Active Directory domain, choose the **Directory User** tab, and log in as a domain user who does not have local administrator permissions on the image builder.

8. Open Internet Explorer and reset your settings by doing the following:

   1. In the upper right area of the Internet Explorer browser window, choose the **Tools** icon, then choose **Internet options**.

   2. Choose the **Advanced **tab, then choose **Reset**.

   3. When prompted to confirm your choice, choose **Reset** again.

   4. When the **Reset Internet Explorer Settings** message displays, choose **Close**.

9. Choose **Admin Commands**, **Switch User**, and then do either of the following:

   - If your image builder is not joined to an Active Directory domain, on the **Local User** tab, choose **Administrator**.
   - If your image builder is joined to an Active Directory domain, choose the **Directory User** tab, and log in with the same domain user account that you used in step 4.

10. On the image builder desktop, open Image Assistant.

11. Follow the necessary steps in Image Assistant to finish creating your image. For more information, see Tutorial: Create a Custom Image.

Change the Default Internet Explorer Home Page for Users' Streaming Sessions

You can use Group Policy to change the default Internet Explorer home page for users' streaming sessions. Alternatively, if you do not have Group Policy in your environment or prefer not to use Group Policy, you can use the AppStream 2.0 Template User account instead.

Topics

- Use Group Policy to Change the Default Internet Explorer Home Page
- Use the AppStream 2.0 Template User Account to Change the Default Internet Explorer Home Page

Use Group Policy to Change the Default Internet Explorer Home Page

In Active Directory environments, you use the Group Policy Management (GPMC) MMC-snap-in to set a default home page that users can't change. If Active Directory is not in your environment, you can use Local Group Policy Editor to perform this task. To set a home page that users can change, you must use the GPMC.

To use the GPMC, do the following first:

- Obtain access to a computer or an EC2 instance that is joined to your domain.
- Install the GPMC. For more information, see Installing or Removing Remote Server Administration Tools for Windows 7 in the Microsoft documentation.
- Log in as a domain user with permissions to create GPOs. Link GPOs to the appropriate organizational units (OUs).

To change the default Internet Explorer home page by using a Group Policy administrative template

You can use a Group Policy administrative template to set a default home page that users can't change. For more information about administrative templates, see Edit Administrative Template Policy Settings in the Microsoft documentation.

1. Open the AppStream 2.0 console at https://console.aws.amazon.com/appstream2.

2. If you are not using Active Directory in your environment, open Local Group Policy Editor. If you are using Active Directory, open the GPMC. Locate the **Scripts (Logon\Logoff) **policy setting:

    - Local Group Policy Editor:

      On your image builder, open the command prompt as an administrator, type `gpedit.msc`, and then press ENTER.

      Under **User Configuration**, expand **Administrative Templates**, **Windows Components**, and then choose **Internet Explorer**.

    - GPMC:

      In your directory or on a domain controller, open the command prompt as an administrator, type `gpmc.msc`, and then press ENTER.

      In the left console tree, select the OU in which you want to create a new GPO, or use an existing GPO, and then do either of the following: :

        - Create a new GPO by opening the context (right-click) menu and choosing **Create a GPO in this domain, Link it here**. For **Name**, provide a descriptive name for this GPO.
        - Select an existing GPO.

      Open the context menu for the GPO, and choose **Edit**.

      Under **User Configuration**, expand **Policies**, **Administrative Templates**, **Windows Components**, and then choose **Internet Explorer**.

3. Double-click **Disable changing home page settings**, choose **Enabled**, and in **Home Page**, enter a URL.

4. Choose **Apply, OK**.

5. Close Local Group Policy Editor or the GPMC.

To change the default Internet Explorer home page by using Group Policy preferences

You can use Group Policy preferences to set a default home page that users can change. For more information about working with Group Policy preferences, see Configure a Registry Item and Group Policy Preferences Getting Started Guide in the Microsoft documentation.

1. In your directory or on a domain controller, open the command prompt as an administrator, type `gpmc.msc`, and then press ENTER.

2. In the left console tree, select the OU in which you want to create a new GPO, or use an existing GPO, and then do either of the following:

    - Create a new GPO by opening the context (right-click) menu and choosing **Create a GPO in this domain, Link it here**. For **Name**, provide a descriptive name for this GPO.
    - Select an existing GPO.

3. Open the context menu for the GPO, and choose **Edit**.

4. Under **User Configuration**, expand **Preferences**, and then choose **Windows Settings**.

5. Open the context (right-click) menu for **Registry** and choose **New, Registry Item**.

6. In the **New Registry Properties** dialog box, specify the following registry settings for Group Policy to configure:

    - For **Action**, choose **Update**.
    - For **Hive**, choose **HKEY_CURRENT_USER**.
    - For **Key Path**, browse to and select HKEY_CURRENT_USER\SOFWARE\Microsoft\Internet Explorer\Main.
    - For **Value Name**, enter **Start Page**.
    - For **Value Data**, enter your home page URL.

7. On the **Common **tab, choose **Apply Once, Do not Re-Apply. Note**
    To enable your users to choose the **Use Default** button in their Internet Explorer browser settings and reset their default home page to your company home page, you can also set a value for Default_Page_URL without choosing **Apply Once** and **Do not Re-Apply**.

8. Choose **OK** and close the GPMC.

Use the AppStream 2.0 Template User Account to Change the Default Internet Explorer Home Page

Follow these steps to use the Template User account to change the default Internet Explorer home page.

To change the default Internet Explorer Home page by using the Template User account

1. Open the AppStream 2.0 console at https://console.aws.amazon.com/appstream2.

2. In the left navigation pane, choose **Images, Image Builder**.

3. Choose the image builder on which to change the default Internet Explorer home page, verify that it is in the **Running** state, and choose **Connect**.

4. Log in to the image builder by doing either of the following:

    - If your image builder is not joined to an Active Directory domain, on the **Local User** tab, choose **Template User**.
    - If your image builder is joined to an Active Directory domain, choose the **Directory User** tab, specify the credentials for a domain user account that does not have local administrator permissions on the image builder, then choose **Log in**.

5. Open Internet Explorer and complete the necessary steps to change the default home page.

6. In the upper right area of the image builder desktop, choose **Admin Commands, Switch User**.

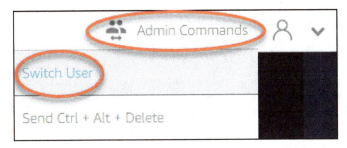

7. This disconnects your current session and opens the login menu. Log in to the image builder by doing either of the following:

   - If your image builder is not joined to an Active Directory domain, on the **Local User** tab, choose **Administrator**.
   - If your image builder is joined to an Active Directory domain, choose the **Directory User** tab, and log in as a domain user who has local administrator permissions on the image builder.

8. On the image builder desktop, open Image Assistant.

9. Follow the necessary steps in Image Assistant to finish creating your image. For more information, see Tutorial: Create a Custom Image.

Fleet Auto Scaling for Amazon AppStream 2.0

Fleet Auto Scaling allows you to automatically change the size of your AppStream 2.0 fleet to match the supply of available instances to user demand. Because each instance in a fleet can be used by only one user at a time, the size of your fleet determines the number of users who can stream concurrently. You can define scaling policies that adjust the size of your fleet automatically based on a variety of utilization metrics, and optimize the number of available instances to match user demand. You can also choose to turn off automatic scaling and make the fleet run at a fixed size.

AppStream 2.0 scaling is provided by Application Auto Scaling. For more information, see the Application Auto Scaling API Reference.

Before you can use Fleet Auto Scaling, Application Auto Scaling needs permissions to access Amazon CloudWatch alarms and AppStream 2.0 fleets. For more information, see IAM Service Roles Required for Managing AppStream 2.0 Resources and Application Auto Scaling Required IAM Permissions.

For a walk-through of AppStream 2.0 scaling, see Scaling Your Desktop Application Streams with Amazon AppStream 2.0 in the *AWS Compute Blog*.

Scaling Concepts

To use Application Auto Scaling effectively, there are a few terms and concepts that you should be familiar with and understand.

Minimum Capacity
The minimum size of the fleet. Scaling policies do not scale your fleet below this value. For example, if you specify 2, your fleet will never have less than 2 instances available. Note that if **Desired Capacity** (set by editing **Fleet Details** and not **Scaling Policies**) is set below the value of **Minimum Capacity** and a scale-out activity is triggered, Application Auto Scaling scales the **Desired Capacity** value up to the value of **Minimum Capacity** and then continues to scale out as required, based on the scaling policy. However, in this example, a scale-in activity does not adjust **Desired Capacity**, because it is already below the **Minimum Capacity** value.

Maximum Capacity
The maximum size of the fleet. Scaling policies do not scale your fleet above this value. For example, if you specify 10, your fleet will never have more than 10 instances available. Note that if **Desired Capacity** (set by editing **Fleet Details** and not **Scaling Policies**) is set above the value of **Maximum Capacity** and a scale-in activity is triggered, Application Auto Scaling scales **Desired Capacity** down to the value of **Maximum Capacity** and then continues to scale in as required, based on the scaling policy. However, in this example, a scale-out activity does not adjust **Desired Capacity**, because it is already above the **Maximum Capacity** value.

Scaling Policy Action
The action that scaling policies perform on your fleet when the **Scaling Policy Condition** is met. You can choose an action based on **% capacity** or **number of instance(s)**. For example, if **Desired Capacity** is 4 and **Scaling Policy Action** is set to "Add 25% capacity", **Desired Capacity** is increased by 25% to 5 when **Scaling Policy Condition** is met.

Scaling Policy Condition
The condition that triggers the action set in **Scaling Policy Action**. This condition includes a scaling policy metric, a comparison operator, and a threshold. For example, to scale a fleet if the utilization of the fleet is greater than 50%, your scaling policy condition should be "If Capacity Utilization > 50%".

Scaling Policy Metric
This is the metric on which your scaling policy is based. The following metrics are available for scaling policies:
Capacity Utilization
Percentage of instances in a fleet that are being used. You can use this metric to scale your fleet based on

usage of the fleet. For example, **Scaling Policy Condition**: "If Capacity Utilization < 25%" perform **Scaling Policy Action**: "Remove 25 % capacity".

Available Capacity

Number of instances in your fleet that are available for user sessions. You can use this metric to maintain a buffer in your capacity available for users to start streaming sessions. For example, **Scaling Policy Condition**: "If Available Capacity < 5" perform **Scaling Policy Action**: "Add 5 instance(s)".

Insufficient Capacity Error

Number of session requests rejected due to lack of capacity. You can use this metric to provision new instances for users that are unable to get sessions because of lack of capacity. For example, **Scaling Policy Condition**: "If Insufficient Capacity Error > 0" perform **Scaling Policy Action**: "Add 1 instance(s)".

Managing Fleet Scaling Using the Console

You can set up and manage fleet scaling using the AWS Management Console in two ways: during fleet creation, or anytime using the **Fleets** tab. Two default scaling policies are associated with newly created fleets after launch and can be edited via the console from the **Scaling Policies** tab. For more information, see Create a Fleet.

For user environments that vary in number, define scaling policies to control how scaling responds to demand. If you expect a fixed number of users or have other reasons for disabling scaling, you can set your fleet with a fixed number of instances.

To set a fleet scaling policy using the console

1. Open the AppStream 2.0 console at https://console.aws.amazon.com/appstream2.

2. In the navigation pane, choose **Fleets**.

3. Select the fleet and then choose **Scaling Policies**.

4. Edit existing policies by choosing the edit icon next to each value. Set the desired values in the edit field and choose **Update**. The policy changes go into effect within a few minutes.

5. Add (create) new policies using the **Add Policy** link. Set the desired values in the edit field and choose **Create**. The new policy goes into effect within a few minutes.

You can use the **Fleet Usage** tab to monitor the effects of your scaling policy changes. The following is an example usage graph of scaling activity when five users connect to the fleet and then disconnect. This example is from a fleet using the following scaling policy values:

- Minimum Capacity = 1
- Maximum Capacity = 5
- Scale Out = Add 2 instances if Capacity Utilization > 75%
- Scale In = Remove 1 instance if Capacity Utilization < 25%

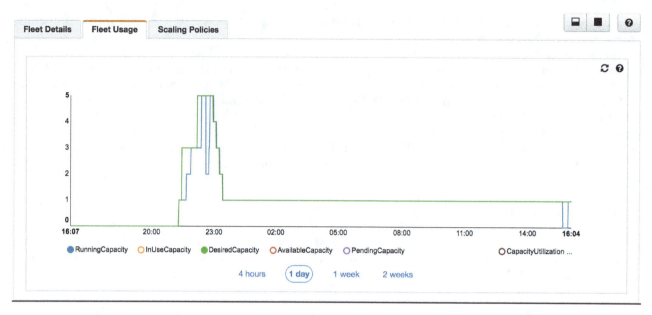

To set a fixed capacity fleet using the console

1. Open the AppStream 2.0 console at https://console.aws.amazon.com/appstream2.

2. In the navigation pane, choose **Fleets**.

3. Select the fleet.

4. For **Scaling Policies**, remove all policies associated with the fleet.

5. For **Fleet Details**, edit the fleet to set **Desired Capacity**.

The fixed fleet has constant capacity based on the value that you specified as **Desired Capacity**. Note that a fixed fleet has the desired number of instances available at all times and the fleet must be stopped to stop billing costs for that fleet.

Managing Fleet Scaling Using the AWS CLI

You can set up and manage fleet scaling using the AWS Command Line Interface (CLI). Before running scaling policy commands, you must register your fleet as a scalable target. Use the following register-scalable-target command:

```
1 aws application-autoscaling register-scalable-target
2     --service-namespace appstream \
3     --resource-id fleet/fleetname \
4     --scalable-dimension appstream:fleet:DesiredCapacity \
5     --min-capacity 1 --max-capacity 5 \
6     --role-arn arn:aws:iam::account-number-without-hyphens:role/service-role/
         ApplicationAutoScalingForAmazonAppStreamAccess
```

Topics

- Example 1: Applying a Scaling Policy Based on Capacity Utilization
- Example 2: Applying a Scaling Policy Based on Insufficient Capacity Errors
- Example 3: Change the Fleet Capacity Based on a Schedule

Example 1: Applying a Scaling Policy Based on Capacity Utilization

This CLI example sets up a scaling policy that scales out a fleet by 25% if Utilization $>= 75\%$.

The following put-scaling-policy command defines a utilization-based scaling policy:

```
1 aws application-autoscaling put-scaling-policy --cli-input-json file://scale-out-utilization.
    json
```

The contents of the file `scale-out-utilization.json` are as follows:

```
1  {
2      "PolicyName": "policyname",
3      "ServiceNamespace": "appstream",
4      "ResourceId": "fleet/fleetname",
5      "ScalableDimension": "appstream:fleet:DesiredCapacity",
6      "PolicyType": "StepScaling",
7      "StepScalingPolicyConfiguration": {
8          "AdjustmentType": "PercentChangeInCapacity",
9          "StepAdjustments": [
10             {
11                 "MetricIntervalLowerBound": 0,
12                 "ScalingAdjustment": 25
13             }
14         ],
15         "Cooldown": 1500
16     }
17 }
```

If the command is successful, the output looks something like the following, although some details are unique to your account and region. In this example, the policy identifier is e3425d21-16f0-d701-89fb-12f98dac64af.

```
1 {"PolicyARN": "arn:aws:autoscaling:us-west-2:123456789012:scalingPolicy:e3425d21-16f0-d701-89fb
    -12f98dac64af:resource/appstream/fleet/SampleFleetName:policyName/SamplePolicyName"}
```

Now, set up a CloudWatch alarm for this policy. Use the names, region, account number, and policy identifier from your information. You can use the policy ARN returned by the previous command for the `--alarm-actions` parameter.

```
1  aws cloudwatch put-metric-alarm
2  --alarm-name alarmname \
3  --alarm-description "Alarm when Capacity Utilization exceeds 75 percent" \
4  --metric-name CapacityUtilization \
5  --namespace AWS/AppStream \
6  --statistic Average \
7  --period 300 \
8  --threshold 75 \
9  --comparison-operator GreaterThanThreshold \
10 --dimensions "Name=FleetName,Value=fleetname" \
11 --evaluation-periods 1 --unit Percent \
12 --alarm-actions "arn:aws:autoscaling:your-region-code:account-number-without-hyphens:
    scalingPolicy:policyid:resource/appstream/fleet/fleetname:policyName/policyname"
```

Example 2: Applying a Scaling Policy Based on Insufficient Capacity Errors

This CLI example sets up a scaling policy that scales out the fleet by 1 if the fleet throws an `InsufficientCapacityError` error.

The following command defines a insufficient capacity-based scaling policy:

```
1 aws application-autoscaling put-scaling-policy --cli-input-json file://scale-out-capacity.json
```

The contents of the file `scale-out-capacity.json` are as follows:

```
1  {
2      "PolicyName": "policyname",
3      "ServiceNamespace": "appstream",
4      "ResourceId": "fleet/fleetname",
5      "ScalableDimension": "appstream:fleet:DesiredCapacity",
6      "PolicyType": "StepScaling",
7      "StepScalingPolicyConfiguration": {
8          "AdjustmentType": "ChangeInCapacity",
9          "StepAdjustments": [
10             {
11                 "MetricIntervalLowerBound": 0,
12                 "ScalingAdjustment": 1
13             }
14         ],
15         "Cooldown": 1500
16     }
17 }
```

If the command is successful, the output looks something like the following, although some details are unique to your account and region. In this example, the policy identifier is `f4495f21-0650-470c-88e6-0f393adb64fc`.

```
1 {"PolicyARN": "arn:aws:autoscaling:us-west-2:123456789012:scalingPolicy:f4495f21-0650-470c-88e6
    -0f393adb64fc:resource/appstream/fleet/SampleFleetName:policyName/SamplePolicyName"}
```

Now, set up a CloudWatch alarm for this policy. Use the names, region, account number, and policy identifier from your information. You can use the policy ARN returned by the previous command for the `--alarm-actions` parameter.

```
1  aws cloudwatch put-metric-alarm
2  --alarm-name alarmname \
3  --alarm-description "Alarm when out of capacity is > 0" \
4  --metric-name InsufficientCapacityError \
5  --namespace AWS/AppStream \
6  --statistic Maximum \
7  --period 300 \
8  --threshold 0 \
9  --comparison-operator GreaterThanThreshold \
10 --dimensions "Name=FleetName,Value=fleetname" \
11 --evaluation-periods 1 --unit Count \
12 --alarm-actions "arn:aws:autoscaling:your-region-code:account-number-without-hyphens:
     scalingPolicy:policyid:resource/appstream/fleet/fleetname:policyName/policyname"
```

Example 3: Change the Fleet Capacity Based on a Schedule

Changing your fleet capacity based on a schedule allows you to scale your fleet capacity in response to predictable changes in demand. For example, at the start of a work day, you might expect a certain number of users to request streaming connections at one time. To change your fleet capacity based on a schedule, you can use the Application Auto Scaling PutScheduledAction API action or the put-scheduled-action CLI command.

Before changing your fleet capacity, you can list your current fleet capacity by using the AppStream 2.0 describe-fleets CLI command.

```
1 aws appstream describe-fleets --name fleetname
```

The current fleet capacity will appear similar to the following output (shown in JSON format):

```
1 {
2     {
3             "ComputeCapacityStatus": {
4                 "Available": 1,
5                 "Desired": 1,
6                 "Running": 1,
7                 "InUse": 0
8             },
9 }
```

Then, use the `put-scheduled-action` command to create a scheduled action to change your fleet capacity. For example, the following command changes the minimum capacity to 3 and the maximum capacity to 5 every day at 9:00 AM.

```
1 aws application-autoscaling put-scheduled-action --service-namespace appstream \
2 --resource-id fleet/fleetname \
3 --schedule="cron(0 9 * * ? *)" \
4 --scalable-target-action MinCapacity=3,MaxCapacity=5 \
5 --scheduled-action-name ExampleScheduledAction \
6 --scalable-dimension appstream:fleet:DesiredCapacity
```

To confirm that the scheduled action to change your fleet capacity was successfully created, run the describe-scheduled-actions command.

```
1 aws application-autoscaling describe-scheduled-actions --service-namespace appstream --resource-
    id fleet/fleetname
```

If the scheduled action was successfully created, the JSON output appears similar to the following.

```
1 {
2     "ScheduledActions": [
3         {
4             "ScalableDimension": "appstream:fleet:DesiredCapacity",
5             "Schedule": "cron(0 9 * * ? *)",
6             "ResourceId": "fleet/ExampleFleet",
7             "CreationTime": 1518651232.886,
8             "ScheduledActionARN": "<arn>",
9             "ScalableTargetAction": {
10                 "MinCapacity": 3,
11                 "MaxCapacity": 5
12             },
13             "ScheduledActionName": "ExampleScheduledAction",
14             "ServiceNamespace": "appstream"
15         }
16     ]
17 }
```

To learn more about creating scheduled actions by using the Application Auto Scaling CLI commands or API actions, see the application-autoscaling section of the AWS CLI Command Reference and Application Auto Scaling API Reference.

Add Your Custom Branding to Amazon AppStream 2.0

To create a familiar experience for your users when they stream applications, you can customize the appearance of AppStream 2.0 with your own branding images, text, and website links, and you can choose from one of several color palettes. When you customize AppStream 2.0, your branding is displayed to users during application streaming sessions rather than the default AppStream 2.0 branding.

Custom Branding Options

You can customize the appearance of the streaming application catalog page by using the following branding options.

Note
Custom branding is not available for the user pool sign-in portal or for the email notifications that AppStream 2.0 sends to user pool users.

Branding element	Description	Requirements and recommendations
Organization logo	Enables you to display an image that is familiar to your users. The image appears in the header of the streaming application catalog page, which is displayed to users after they sign in to AppStream 2.0.	File type: .png, jpg, .jpeg, or .gif Maximum dimensions: 1000 px x 500 px Maximum file size: 300 KB
Organization website links	Enables you to display links to helpful resources for your users, such as your organization's IT support and product marketing sites. The links are displayed in the footer of the streaming application catalog page.	Maximum number of links: 3 Format (URL): https://example/.com or http://example/.com Maximum length (display name): 100 letters, spaces, and numbers Special characters allowed (display name): @ . / # & + $
Color theme	Applied to website links, text, and buttons. These colors are also applied as accents in the background for the streaming application catalog page.	Predefined themes from which to choose: 4 For information about each color theme, see Color Theme Palettes later in this topic.
Page title	Displayed at the top of the browser tab during users' application streaming sessions.	Maximum length: 200 letters, spaces, and numbers. Special characters allowed: @ . / # & + $
Favicon	Enables your users to recognize their application streaming site in a browser full of tabs or bookmarks. The favicon icon is displayed at the top of the browser tab for the application streaming site during users' streaming sessions.	File type: .png, .jpg, .jpeg, .gif, or .ico Maximum dimensions: 128 px x 128 px Maximum file size: 50 KB

Branding element	Description	Requirements and recommendations
Redirect URL	Enables you to specify a URL to which users are redirected when they end a streaming session.	Format: https://example/.com or http://example/.com This URL is configured in the **Details** page for a stack when you create or edit a stack, not in the **Branding** page.
Feedback URL	Enables you to specify a URL for a Send Feedback link, so that your users can submit feedback. If you do not specify a URL, the Send Feedback link is not displayed.	Format: https://example/.com or http://example/.com This URL is configured in the **Details** page for a stack when you create or edit a stack, not in the **Branding** page.

Adding Your Custom Branding to AppStream 2.0

To customize AppStream 2.0 with your organizational branding, use the AppStream 2.0 console to select the stack to customize, and then add your branding.

To add your custom branding to AppStream 2.0

1. Open the AppStream 2.0 console at https://console.aws.amazon.com/appstream2.

2. In the left pane, choose **Stacks**.

3. In the stack list, select the stack to customize with your branding.

4. Choose **Branding**, **Custom**.

5. For **Application catalog page**, customize how the streaming application catalog page appears to users after they sign in to AppStream 2.0.

    1. For **Organization logo**, do either of the following:

        - If you are uploading a logo for the first time, choose **Upload**, and then select the image to display in the header of the streaming application catalog page.
        - If you have already uploaded a logo and need to change it, choose **Change Logo**, and then select the image to display.

    2. For **Organization website links**, specify up to three website links to display in the page footer. For each link, choose the **Add Link **button, and then enter a display name and URL. To add more links, repeat these steps for each link to add. To remove a link, choose the **Remove **button under the link URL.

    3. For **Color theme**, choose the colors to use for your website links, body text, and buttons, and as an accent for the page background. For information about each color theme, see Color Theme Palettes later in this topic.

6. For **Browser tab**, customize the page title and icon to display to users at the top of their browser tab during streaming sessions.

    1. For **Page title**, enter the title to display at the top of the browser tab.

    2. For **Favicon**, do either of the following:

        - If you are uploading a favicon for the first time, choose **Upload**, and then select the image to display at the top of the browser tab.
        - If you have already uploaded a favicon and want to change it, choose **Change Logo**, and then select the image to display.

7. Do either of the following:

- To apply your branding changes, choose **Save**. When users connect to new streaming sessions that are launched for the stack, your branding changes are displayed. **Note**
AppStream 2.0 retains the custom branding changes that you save. If you save your custom branding changes, but then choose to restore the AppStream 2.0 default branding, your custom branding changes are saved for later use. If you restore the AppStream 2.0 default branding and decide later to reapply your custom branding, choose **Custom**, **Save**. In this case, the most recently saved custom branding is displayed to your users.
- To discard your branding changes, choose **Cancel**. When prompted to confirm your choice, choose **Confirm**. If you cancel your changes, the most recently saved branding is displayed to your users.

Specifying a Custom Redirect URL and Feedback URL

You can specify a URL to which your users are redirected when they end their streaming session, as well as a URL where your users can submit feedback. By default, AppStream 2.0 displays a **Send Feedback** link that enables users to submit feedback to AWS about the quality of their application streaming session. To enable your users to submit feedback to a site that you specify, you can provide a custom feedback URL. You can specify the redirect URL and feedback URL when you create a new stack or edit the details for an existing stack. For more information, see Create a Stack.

Previewing Your Custom Branding Changes

You can preview how your branding changes will appear to your users by applying your branding changes to a test stack before you apply them to a production stack, and then creating a streaming URL for the test stack. After you validate your branding changes, you can them deploy them to your production stack. For information, see Step 2: Provide Access to Users in *Getting Started with Amazon AppStream 2.0*.

Color Theme Palettes

When you choose a color theme, the colors for that theme are applied to the website links, text, and buttons in your streaming application catalog page. A color is also applied as an accent in the background for your streaming application catalog page. For each color in a color theme palette, the hex value is also noted.

Topics

- Red
- Light Blue
- Blue
- Pink

Red

The following colors are applied when you select the red color theme.

Red (#d51900) – Used for buttons and website links.

White (#faf9f7) – Used as a background accent.

Dark grey (#404040) – Used for the body text and in the progress spinner.

When you choose the red color theme, the website links, body text, and background accent appear in your streaming application catalog page as follows.

Choose your app to get started

firefox   node   notepad

Products | About us
© Powered by Amazon AppStream 2.0
aws

Light Blue

The following colors are applied when you select the light blue color theme:

Light blue (#1d83c2) – Used for buttons and website links.

White (#f6f6f6) – Used as a background accent.

Dark grey (#333333) – Used for the body text and in the progress spinner.

When you choose the light blue color theme, the website links, body text, and background accent appear in your streaming application catalog page as follows.

Choose your app to get started

firefox   node   notepad

Products | About us
© Powered by Amazon AppStream 2.0
aws

Blue

The following colors are applied when you select the blue color theme:

Blue (#0070ba) – Used for website links.

White (#ffffff) – Used as a background accent.

Light green (#8ac53e) – Used for buttons.

Grey (#666666) – Used for the body text and in the progress spinner.

When you choose the blue color theme, the website links, body text, and background accent appear in your streaming application catalog page as follows.

Choose your app to get started

firefox   node   notepad

Products | About us
© Powered by Amazon AppStream 2.0
aws

Pink

The following colors are applied when you select the pink color theme:

Pink (#ec0069) – Used for website links.

White (#ffffff) – Used as a background accent.

Blue (#3159a2) – Used for buttons.

Dark grey (#333333) – Used for the body text and in the progress spinner.

When you choose the pink color theme, the website links, body text, and background accent appear in your streaming application catalog page as follows.

Choose your app to get started

firefox   node   notepad

Products | About us

© Powered by Amazon AppStream 2.0

Enable Persistent Storage for Your AppStream 2.0 Users

Amazon AppStream 2.0 supports persistent storage for your users with home folders and Google Drive. As an AppStream 2.0 administrator, you must understand how to perform the following tasks to enable and administer persistent storage for your users.

Topics

- Enable and Administer Home Folders for Your AppStream 2.0 Users
- Enable and Administer Google Drive for Your AppStream 2.0 Users

Enable and Administer Home Folders for Your AppStream 2.0 Users

AppStream 2.0 supports persistent storage for your users with home folders and Google Drive. You can enable one or both options as needed for your organization. When you enable home folders for an AppStream 2.0 stack, end users of the stack can access a persistent storage folder during their application streaming sessions. No further configuration is required on your users' part to access their home folder. Data stored by users in their home folder is automatically backed up to an Amazon S3 bucket in your AWS account and is made available in subsequent sessions for those users.

Note

As an administrator, you can access a home folder in the following default location on an image builder instance: C:\Users\PhotonUser\My Files\Home Folder. Use this path if you are configuring your applications to save to the home folder. In some cases, your end users may not be able to find their home folder because some applications do not recognize the redirect that displays the home folder as a top-level folder in File Explorer. If this is the case, your users can access their home folder by browsing to the same directory in File Explorer.

Topics

- Enable Home Folders for Your AppStream 2.0 Users
- Administer Your Home Folders
- Provide Your AppStream 2.0 Users with Guidance for Working with Home Folders

Enable Home Folders for Your AppStream 2.0 Users

Before enabling home folders, you must do the following:

- Check that you have the correct IAM permissions for Amazon S3 actions. For more information, see IAM Policies and the Amazon S3 Bucket for Home Folders.
- Use an image that was created from an AWS base image released on or after May 18, 2017. For a current list of released AWS images, see Amazon AppStream 2.0 Windows Image Version History.
- Enable network connectivity to Amazon S3 from your VPC by configuring internet access or a VPC endpoint for Amazon S3. For more information, see Network Settings for Amazon AppStream 2.0 and Home Folders and VPC Endpoints.

You can enable or disable home folders while creating a stack (see Create a Stack), or after the stack is created by using the AWS Management Console for AppStream 2.0, AWS SDK, or AWS CLI. For each AWS Region, home folders are backed up by an S3 bucket.

The first time you enable home folders for an AppStream 2.0 stack in an AWS Region, the service creates an S3 bucket in your account in that same region. The same bucket is used to store the content of home folders for all users and all stacks in that region. For more information, see Amazon S3 Bucket Storage.

To enable home folders while creating a stack

- Follow the steps in Create a Stack, and ensure that **Enable Home Folders** is selected.

To enable home folders for an existing stack

1. Open the AppStream 2.0 console at https://console.aws.amazon.com/appstream2.

2. On the left navigation pane, choose **Stacks**, and select the stack for which to enable home folders.

3. Below the stacks list, choose **Storage** and select **Enable Home Folders**.

4. In the **Enable Home Folders** dialog box, choose **Enable**.

Administer Your Home Folders

Topics

- Disable Home Folders
- Amazon S3 Bucket Storage
- Home Folder Formats
- Using the AWS Command Line Interface or AWS SDKs

Disable Home Folders

You can disable home folders for a stack without losing user content already stored in home folders. Disabling home folders for a stack has the following effects:

- For any users who are connected to active streaming sessions for the stack, an error message displays during the session to inform these users that they can no longer store content in their home folder.
- Any new sessions that use the stack with home folders disabled do not present home folders.
- Disabling home folders for one stack does not disable it for other stacks. Only the specific stack for which home folders is disabled is affected.
- Even if home folders are disabled for all stacks, AppStream 2.0 does not delete the user content.

To restore access to home folders for the stack, enable home folders again by following the steps described earlier in this topic.

To disable home folders while creating a stack

- Follow the steps in Create a Stack and ensure that **Enable Home Folders** is cleared.

To disable home folders for an existing stack

1. Open the AppStream 2.0 console at https://console.aws.amazon.com/appstream2.

2. On the left navigation pane, choose **Stacks**, and select the stack.

3. Below the stacks list, choose **Storage** and clear **Enable Home Folders**.

4. In the **Disable Home Folders** dialog box, type CONFIRM (case-sensitive) to confirm your choice, then choose **Disable**.

Amazon S3 Bucket Storage

AppStream 2.0 manages user content stored in home folders by using S3 buckets created in your account. For every region, AppStream 2.0 creates a bucket in your account and stores all user content generated from streaming sessions of stacks in that region in that bucket. The buckets are fully managed by the service without any admin inputs or configuration. The buckets are named in a specific format as follows:

```
1  appstream2-36fb080bb8-region-code-account-id-without-hyphens
```

Where `region-code` is the AWS region code in which the stack is created and `account-id-without-hyphens` is your AWS account ID. The first part of the bucket name, `appstream2-36fb080bb8-`, does not change across accounts or regions.

For example, if you enable home folders for stacks in region us-west-2 on account number 123456789012, the service creates an S3 bucket in the us-west-2 region with the name shown. This bucket name cannot change or be deleted without manual modification by an administrator.

```
1  appstream2-36fb080bb8-us-west-2-123456789012
```

As mentioned, disabling home folders for stacks does not delete any user content stored in the S3 bucket. To permanently delete user content, an administrator with adequate access must do so from the Amazon S3 console. AppStream 2.0 adds a bucket policy that prevents accidental deletion of the bucket. For more information, see IAM Policies and the Amazon S3 Bucket for Home Folders.

Additional Resources

To learn more about managing S3 buckets and best practices, see the following topics in the *Amazon Simple Storage Service Developer Guide*:

- You can provide offline access to user data for your users with Amazon S3 policies. For more information, see Allow Users to Access a Personal "Home Directory" in Amazon S3.
- You can enable file versioning for content stored in S3 buckets used by AppStream 2.0. For more information, see Using Versioning.

Home Folder Formats

When home folders are enabled, users are provided with a unique folder in which to store their content (one folder per user). The folder is created and maintained as a unique Amazon S3 object within the bucket for that region. The hierarchy of a user folder depends on how the user launches a streaming session.

AWS SDKs and AWS CLI

For sessions created using `CreateStreamingURL` or `create-streaming-url` the user folder structure is as follows:

```
1 bucket-name/user/custom/user-id-SHA-256-hash/
```

Where `bucket-name` is in the format shown in Amazon S3 Bucket Storage and `user-id-SHA-256-hash` is the user-specific folder name created using a lower case SHA-256 hash hexadecimal string generated from the `UserId` value passed to the CreateStreamingURL API operation or `create-streaming-url` command. For more information, see CreateStreamingURL in the *Amazon AppStream 2.0 API Reference* and create-streaming-url in the *AWS CLI Command Reference*.

The following example folder structure applies to session access using the API or CLI with a `UserId` testuser@mydomain.com, account id 123456789012 in region us-west-2:

```
1 appstream2-36fb080bb8-us-west-2-123456789012/user/custom/
    a0bcb1da11f480d9b5b3e90f91243143eac04cfccfbdc777e740fab628a1cd13/
```

Administrators can identify the folder for a user by generating the lower case SHA-256 hash value of the `UserId` using websites or open source coding libraries available online.

SAML

For sessions created using SAML federation, the user folder structure is as follows:

```
1 bucket-name/user/federated/user-id-SHA-256-hash/
```

In this case, `user-id-SHA-256-hash` is the folder name created using a lower case SHA-256 hash hexadecimal string generated from the `NameID` SAML attribute value passed in the SAML federation request. To differentiate users with the same name belonging to two different domains, send the SAML request with `NameID` in the format `domainname\username`. For more information, see Single Sign-on Access to AppStream 2.0 Using SAML 2.0.

The following example folder structure applies to session access using SAML federation with a `NameID` SAMPLE-DOMAIN\testuser, account ID 123456789012 in region us-west-2:

```
1 appstream2-36fb080bb8-us-west-2-123456789012/user/federated/34832
    ec7383294b01bface2ebc32ab9cacfb5fc12ad33d5eb5d0fcc1d78ae144
```

When part or all of the NameID string is capitalized (as the domain name *SAMPLEDOMAIN* is in the example), AppStream 2.0 converts the string to lowercase and then generates the hash value based on the lowercase string. So for the example, AppStream 2.0 converts the `NameID` string *SAMPLEDOMAIN\test user* to *sampledomain\testuser* and generates the hash value based on that string. Administrators can identify the folder for a user by generating the SHA-256 hash value of the lowercase `NameID` by using websites or open source coding libraries available online.

Using the AWS Command Line Interface or AWS SDKs

You can enable and disable home folders for a stack using the AWS CLI or AWS SDKs.

Use the following create-stack command enable home folders while creating a new stack:

```
1 aws appstream create-stack --name ExampleStack --storage-connectors type=HOMEFOLDERS
```

Use the following update-stack command to enable home folders for an existing stack:

```
1 aws appstream update-stack --name ExistingStack --storage-connectors type=HOMEFOLDERS
```

Use the following command to disable home folders for an existing stack. This command does not delete any user data.

```
1 aws appstream update-stack -name ExistingStack --delete-storage-connectors
```

Provide Your AppStream 2.0 Users with Guidance for Working with Home Folders

To help your users understand how to work with home folders, you can provide them with the following information.

Guidance for Users

When you are signed in to an AppStream 2.0 streaming session, you can do the following with your home folder:

- Open and edit files and folders that you store in your home folder. Content that is stored in your home folder is specific to you and cannot be accessed by other users.
- Upload and download files between your local computer and your home folder. AppStream 2.0 continuously checks for the most recently modified files and folders and backs them up to your home folder.
- When you are working in an application, you can access files and folders that are stored in your home folder by choosing **File Open** from the application interface and browsing to the file or folder that you want to open. To save changes to a file that you are working in to your home folder, choose **File Save** from the application interface and browse to the location in your home folder where you want to save the file.
- You can also access your home folder by choosing **My Files** from the web view session toolbar. **Note** If your home folder doesn't appear, you can view your home folder files by browsing to the following directory in File Explorer: C:\Users\PhotonUser\My Files\Home Folder.

To upload and download files between your local computer and your home folder

1. In the AppStream 2.0 web view session, choose the **My Files** icon at the top left of your browser.

2. Navigate to an existing folder, or choose **Add Folder** to create a new folder.

3. When the folder that you want is displayed, do one of the following:

   - To upload a file to the folder, select the file that you want to upload, and choose **Upload**.

- To download a file from the folder, select the file that you want to download, choose the down arrow to the right of the file name, and choose **Download**.

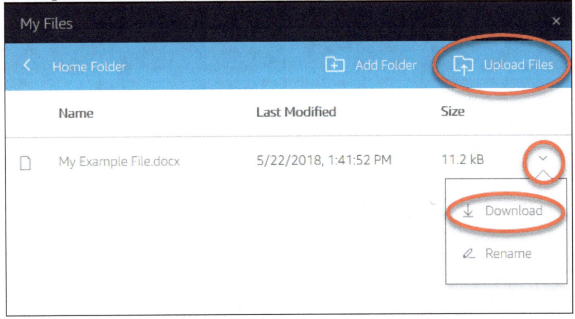

Enable and Administer Google Drive for Your AppStream 2.0 Users

AppStream 2.0 supports persistent storage for your users with Google Drive and home folders. You can enable one or both options as needed for your organization. When you enable Google Drive for an AppStream 2.0 stack, end users of the stack can link their Google Drive account to AppStream 2.0. After their account is linked to AppStream 2.0, your users can sign into their Google Drive account and access their Google Drive folder during application streaming sessions. Any changes that your users make to files or folders in their Google Drive during application streaming sessions are automatically backed up and synchronized so that they are available to users outside their streaming session.

Important
You can enable Google Drive for accounts in G Suite domains only, not for personal Gmail accounts.

Topics

- Enable Google Drive for Your AppStream 2.0 Users
- Disable Google Drive for Your AppStream 2.0 Users
- Provide Your AppStream 2.0 Users with Guidance for Working with Google Drive

Enable Google Drive for Your AppStream 2.0 Users

Before enabling Google Drive, you must do the following:

- Make sure that the stack on which you enable Google Drive is associated with a fleet based on an image that uses a version of the AppStream 2.0 agent released on or after May 31, 2018. For more information, see Amazon AppStream 2.0 Agent Version History. The fleet must also have access to the internet.
- Add Amazon AppStream 2.0 as a trusted app in one or more G Suite domains. You can enable Google Drive for up to 10 G Suite domains.

Follow these steps to add Amazon AppStream 2.0 as a trusted app in your G Suite domains.

To add Amazon AppStream 2.0 as a trusted app in your G Suite domains

1. Sign in to the G Suite Admin console at https://admin.google.com/.

2. Choose **Dashboard**.

3. Choose the main menu in the upper left of the window (to the left of the **Google Admin** title), then choose **Security, Settings**.

4. Choose **API Permissions**.

5. At the bottom of the **API Access** list, choose the **Trusted Apps** link.

6. Choose the **Whitelist an App** [plus sign (+) icon] in the bottom right of the window.

7. In the **Add APP to Trusted List** dialog box, do the following. When you're done, choose **Add**:

    - For **Select App Type**, choose **Web Application**.
    - For **OAuth2 Client ID**, type the Amazon AppStream 2.0 OAuth client ID for your AWS Region. For a list of client IDs, see the table that follows this procedure.

8. Confirm that Amazon AppStream 2.0 appears in the list of trusted apps.

Amazon AppStream 2.0 OAuth2 client IDs

Region	Amazon AppStream 2.0 OAuth client ID
us-east-1 (N.Virginia)	266080779488-15n5q5nkiclp6m524qibnmhmbsg0hk92.apps.g...
us-west-2 (Oregon)	1026466167591-i4jmemrggsjomp9tnkkcs5tniggfiujb.apps.goo...
ap-northeast-1 (Tokyo)	922579247628-qpl9kpihg3hu5dul2lphbjs4qbg6mjm2.apps.goo...

Region	Amazon AppStream 2.0 OAuth client ID
ap-southeast-1 (Singapore)	856871139998-4eia2n1db5j6gtv4c1rdte1fh1gec8vs.apps.googl
ap-southeast-2 (Sydney)	151535156524-b889372osskprm4dt1clpm53mo3m9omp.apps.
eu-central-1 (Frankfurt)	643727794574-1se5360a77i84je9j3ap12obov1ib76q.apps.goog
eu-west-1 (Ireland)	599492309098-098muc7ofjfo9vua5rm5u9q2k3mlok3j.apps.goo

Follow these steps to enable Google Drive for your AppStream 2.0 users.

To enable Google Drive while creating a stack

- Follow the steps in Create a Stack, and ensure that **Enable Google Drive** is selected and that you have specified at least one G Suite domain.

To enable Google Drive for an existing stack

1. Open the AppStream 2.0 console at https://console.aws.amazon.com/appstream2.

2. In the left navigation pane, choose **Stacks**, and select the stack for which to enable Google Drive.

3. Below the stacks list, choose **Storage** and select **Enable Google Drive**.

4. In the **Enable Google Drive** dialog box, in **G Suite domain name**, type the name of at least one G Suite domain. To specify another domain, choose **Add another domain**, and type the name of the G Suite domain.

5. After you finish adding G Suite domain names, choose **Enable**.

Disable Google Drive for Your AppStream 2.0 Users

You can disable Google Drive for a stack without losing user content that is already stored on Google Drive. Disabling Google Drive for a stack has the following effects:

- For any users who are connected to active streaming sessions for the stack, an error message displays during the session to inform these users that they do not have permissions to access their Google Drive.
- Any new sessions that use the stack with Google Drive disabled do not display Google Drive.
- Disabling Google Drive for one stack does not disable it for other stacks. Only the specific stack for which Google Drive is disabled is affected.
- Even if Google Drive is disabled for all stacks, AppStream 2.0 does not delete the user content.

Follow these steps to disable Google Drive for an existing stack.

To disable Google Drive for an existing stack

1. Open the AppStream 2.0 console at https://console.aws.amazon.com/appstream2.

2. In the left navigation pane, choose **Stacks**, and select the stack for which to disable Google Drive.

3. Below the stacks list, choose **Storage** and clear **Enable Google Drive**.

4. In the **Disable Google Drive** dialog box, type CONFIRM (case-sensitive) to confirm your choice, then choose **Disable**.

Provide Your AppStream 2.0 Users with Guidance for Working with Google Drive

To help your users understand how to work with Google Drive, you can provide them with the following information.

Guidance for Users

When you add your Google Drive account to AppStream 2.0 and you are signed in to an AppStream 2.0 streaming session, you can do the following with your Google Drive:

- Open and edit files and folders that you store in your Google Drive. Content that is stored in your Google Drive is specific to you and cannot be accessed by other users unless you choose to share it.
- Upload and download files between your local computer and your Google Drive. Any changes that you make to files and folders in your Google Drive during a streaming session are automatically backed up and synchronized so that they are available to you when you sign in to your Google account and access Google Drive outside your streaming session.
- When you are working in an application, you can access files and folders that are stored in your Google Drive by choosing **File Open** from the application interface and browsing to the file or folder that you want to open. To save changes to a file that you are working in to your Google Drive, choose **File Save** from the application interface and browse to the location in your home folder where you want to save the file.
- You can also access your Google Drive by choosing **My Files** from the web view session toolbar.

To add your Google Drive account to AppStream 2.0

To access your Google Drive during AppStream 2.0 streaming sessions, you must first add your Google Drive account to AppStream 2.0.

1. In the AppStream 2.0 web view session, choose the **My Files** icon at the top left of your browser.

2. In the **My Files** dialog box, choose **Add Google Drive**.

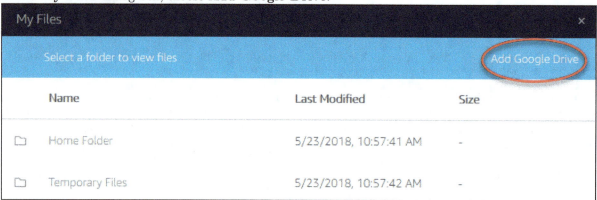

3. Choose the domain for your Google Drive account.

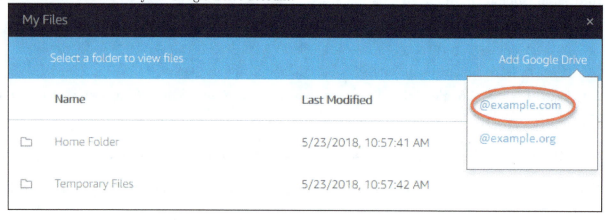

4. The **Sign in with Google** dialog box displays. Enter the user name and password for your Google Drive account when prompted.

5. After your Google Drive account is added to AppStream 2.0, your Google Drive folder displays in **My Files**.

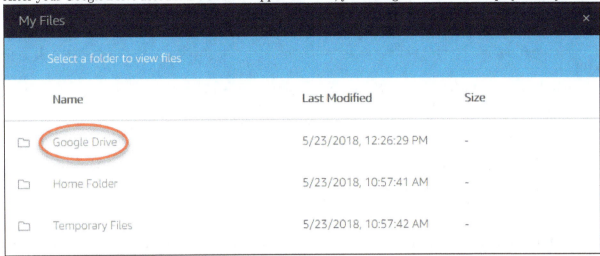

6. To work with files and folders in your Google Drive, choose the **Google Drive** folder and browse to a folder or file as needed. If you do not want to work with files in your Google Drive during this streaming session, close the **My Files** dialog box.

To upload and download files between your local computer and your Google Drive

1. In the AppStream 2.0 web view session, choose the **My Files** icon at the top left of your browser.

2. In the **My Files** dialog box, choose **Google Drive**.

3. Navigate to an existing folder, or choose **Add Folder** to create a new folder.

4. When the folder that you want displays, do one of the following:

   - To upload a file to the folder, select the file that you want to upload, and choose **Upload**.
   - To download a file from the folder, select the file that you want to download, choose the down arrow to the right of the file name, and choose **Download**.

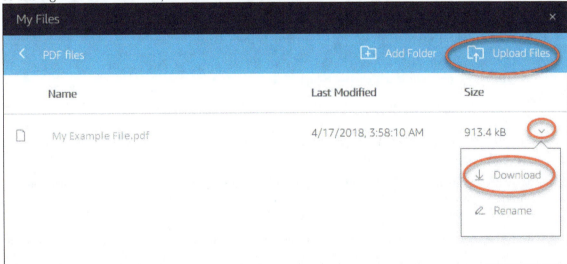

Enable Regional Settings for Your AppStream 2.0 Users

Amazon AppStream 2.0 regional settings enable your users to configure their AppStream 2.0 streaming sessions to use settings that are specific to their location or language. In particular, users can configure the following settings:

- **Time zone** — Determines the system time used by Windows and any applications that rely on the operating system time. AppStream 2.0 makes available the same options for this setting as Windows Server 2012 R2.
- **Locale** (also known as culture) — Determines the conventions used by Windows and any applications that query the Windows culture when formatting dates, numbers, or currencies or when sorting strings. AppStream 2.0 supports the following locales: Chinese (Simplified and Traditional), Dutch, English, French, German, Italian, Japanese, Korean, Portuguese, Spanish, and Thai.
- **Input method** — Determines the keystroke combinations that can be used to input characters in another language.

If users change regional settings during their streaming sessions, the changes are applied to any future streaming sessions in the same AWS Region.

Topics

- Enable Regional Settings for Your AppStream 2.0 Users
- Provide Your AppStream 2.0 Users with Guidance for Working with Regional Settings

Enable Regional Settings for Your AppStream 2.0 Users

To enable users to configure regional settings for a given stack during their AppStream 2.0 streaming sessions, your stack must be associated with a fleet based on an image that uses a version of the AppStream 2.0 agent released on or after June 6, 2018. For more information, see Amazon AppStream 2.0 Agent Version History. Additionally, your image must have Windows PowerShell 5.1 or later installed. Images created from AppStream 2.0 base images published on or after June 12, 2018 meet both criteria. Images created from AppStream 2.0 base images published before June 12, 2018 do not have Windows PowerShell 5.1 by default.

To update an existing image to include Windows PowerShell 5.1

1. Launch a new image builder using your existing image as the base image by doing the following:

   1. In the left navigation pane in the AppStream 2.0 console, choose **Images**.

   2. Choose the **Image Builder** tab, **Launch Image Builder**, and then select your existing image.

   3. If you are prompted to update the AppStream 2.0 agent when you launch the image builder, select the check box, and then choose **Start**.

2. Once your new image builder is running, connect to it and log in with a user account that has local administrator permissions.

3. From the image builder desktop, open Windows PowerShell. Choose the Windows **Start** button, and then choose **Windows PowerShell**.

4. At the PowerShell command prompt, type the command $PSVersionTable to determine the version of Windows PowerShell that is installed on your image builder. If your image builder does not include Windows PowerShell 5.1 or later, use the following steps to install it.

5. Open a web browser and follow the steps in Install and Configure WMF 5.1 in the Microsoft documentation, making sure that you download the Windows Management Framework (WMF) 5.1 package for Windows Server 2012 R2. WMF 5.1 includes Windows PowerShell 5.1.

6. At the end of the WMF 5.1 installation process, the installer prompts you to restart your computer. Choose** Restart Now** to restart the image builder.

7. Wait about 10 minutes before logging in to your image builder, even though AppStream 2.0 prompts you to do so immediately. Otherwise, you might encounter an error.

8. After logging in to your image builder again, open Windows PowerShell and type the command `$PSVersionTable` to confirm that Windows PowerShell 5.1 is installed on your image builder.

9. Use the image builder to create a new image. This new image now includes the latest versions of the AppStream 2.0 agent and Windows PowerShell.

10. Update your fleet to use the new image by doing the following:

    1. In the left navigation pane in the AppStream 2.0 console, choose **Fleets**, and then choose the fleet associated with the stack for which you want to enable regional settings.

    2. On the **Fleet Details** tab, choose **Edit**.

    3. In **Image name,** choose the new image to use for the fleet.

For more information about using image builders to create images, see Tutorial: Create a Custom Image.

Provide Your AppStream 2.0 Users with Guidance for Working with Regional Settings

To help your users understand how to work with regional settings during their streaming sessions, you can provide them with the following information.

Guidance for Users

You can configure regional settings so that your AppStream 2.0 streaming sessions use settings that are specific to your location or language. Changes that you make during your streaming session are applied to future streaming sessions.

To configure regional settings for your AppStream 2.0 streaming sessions

1. In your AppStream 2.0 session, in the top left area, choose the **Settings** icon, and then choose **Regional settings**.

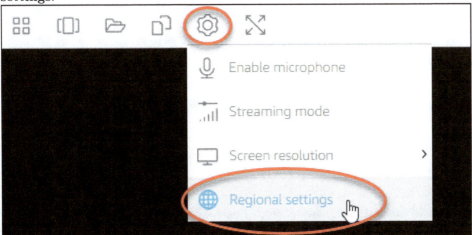

2. In the **Regional settings** dialog box, set the following options as needed. When you're done, choose **Save**.

   - **Time zone** — Determines the system time used by Windows and any applications that rely on the operating system time.
   - **Locale** (also known as culture) — Determines how Windows displays numbers, currency, time, and dates. AppStream 2.0 supports the following locales: Chinese (Simplified and Traditional), Dutch, English, French, German, Italian, Japanese, Korean, Portuguese, Spanish, and Thai.

- **Input method** — Determines the keystroke combinations that can be used to input characters in another language.

Manage Access Using the AppStream 2.0 User Pool

The AppStream 2.0 user pool offers a simplified way to manage access to applications for your end users through a persistent portal for each region. This feature is offered as a built-in alternative to user management through Active Directory and SAML 2.0 federation. To use external identity providers for user management, see Single Sign-on Access to AppStream 2.0 Using SAML 2.0. To join your Active Directory domain to AppStream 2.0, see Using Active Directory with AppStream 2.0.

Note
User pool users cannot be assigned to stacks with fleets that are joined to an Active Directory domain.

The AppStream 2.0 user pool offers the following key features:

- Users can access application stacks through a persistent URL and login credentials using their email address and a password that they choose.
- Administrators can assign a user multiple stacks, offering multiple application catalogs to the user when they log in.
- When an administrator creates a new user, a welcome email is automatically sent to the end user with a login portal link and instructions.
- After being created, a user in the pool remains valid and usable unless an administrator specifically disables that user.
- Administrators can control which users have access to which application stacks, or disable access completely.

User Pool End User Experience

With the user pool, the following flow of actions summarizes the initial connection experience for the end user.

1. An administrator creates a new user in the desired region using the end user's email address.

2. AppStream 2.0 sends a welcome email with instructions and a temporary password.

3. An administrator assigns the user one or more stacks.

4. AppStream 2.0 sends an optional notification email to the end user with information and instructions for the stacks to which the user is newly assigned.

5. Using the information in the welcome email, the end user connects to the login portal and uses their temporary password to set a permanent password. The login portal link never expires and can be used anytime.

6. Using the email address and permanent password they set up earlier, the end user signs in and is presented with their application catalogs.

The login portal link provided in the welcome email should be saved for future use, as it does not change and is valid for all user pool users. Note that the login portal URL and user pool user are managed on a per-region basis.

Resetting a Forgotten Password

If a user forgets their password, they can connect to the login portal link (provided in the welcome email) to choose a new password.

To choose a new password

1. Open the AppStream 2.0 login portal using the login link provided in the welcome email.

2. Choose **Forgot Password?**.

3. Type the email address used to create your user pool user. Choose **Next**.

4. Check your email for the password reset request message. If you are having difficulty finding the email, check your spam email folder. Type the verification code from the email in **Verification Code**. **Note** The verification code is valid for 24 hours. If a new password is not chosen within this time, request a new verification code.

5. Following the password rules shown, type and confirm your new password. Choose **Reset Password**.

User Pool Administration

To perform administrator actions, sign in to the AppStream 2.0 console in the AWS Management Console for the desired region and select User Pool in the left navigation pane. The User Pool dashboard supports bulk operations on a list of users for some actions. An administrator can select multiple users on which to perform the same action from the **Actions** list. Bulk user creation or disable is not supported. User pool users are created and managed on a per-region basis.

Note
AppStream 2.0 sends email to users on your behalf, such as when a new user is created or a user is assigned to a stack. To ensure that email is delivered, add `no-reply@accounts.aws-region-code.amazonappstream.com` to your whitelist, where `aws-region-code` is a valid AWS region code in which you are working. If users are having difficulty finding the emails, ask them to check their "spam" email folder.

Topics

- Creating a User
- Assigning Stacks to Users
- Unassigning Stacks from Users
- Disabling Users
- Enabling Users
- Re-Sending Welcome Email

Creating a User

Users are managed on a per-region basis. You must use a valid and unique email address for each new user within a region. However, you can reuse an email address for a new user in another region.

When you create a new user, be aware of the following:

- There is no limit on the number of users in the user pool.
- You can enable or disable a user, but you cannot delete a user.
- You cannot change the email address, first name, or last name for a user that you have already created. To change this information for a user, disable the user. Then, recreate the user (as a new user) and specify the updated information as needed.
- You can assign one or more stacks to the user after the user is created.

To create a new user

1. Open the AppStream 2.0 console at https://console.aws.amazon.com/appstream2.

2. On the left navigation pane, choose **User Pool**, **Create User**.

3. For **Email**, type the unique email address for this user.

4. For **First name** and **Last name**, type values. These fields need not be unique.

5. Choose **Create User**.

After the user is created, AppStream 2.0 sends a welcome email to the user. This email has the login portal link, the login email address to be used, and a temporary password. By browsing to the login portal and using the temporary password, the user can set a permanent password to access their applications.

By default, the new user's status is **Enabled**, meaning you can assign one or more stacks to the user, or perform other actions.

Assigning Stacks to Users

An AppStream 2.0 administrator can assign one or more stacks to one or more user pool users. After being assigned at least one stack, the user can log in and launch applications. If users are assigned more than one stack, they are presented with a list of stacks as catalogs to choose from before launching applications. User Pool users cannot be assigned to stacks with fleets that are joined to an Active Directory domain.

To assign a stack to users

1. Open the AppStream 2.0 console at https://console.aws.amazon.com/appstream2.

2. On the left navigation pane, choose **User Pool** and select the users.

3. Choose **Actions, Assign stack**. Note that users cannot be assigned to stacks that have a fleet joined to an Active Directory domain. For more information, see Using Active Directory with AppStream 2.0.

4. Confirm the list of users in the resulting dialog box. For **Stack**, choose the desired stack.

5. By default, **Send email notification to user** is enabled. Clear this option if you do not want to send the notification email to the user at this time.

6. Choose **Assign stack**.

Unassigning Stacks from Users

An AppStream 2.0 administrator can unassign stacks from one or more user pool users. After being unassigned a stack, the user can no longer launch applications from that stack.

To unassign a stack from users

1. Open the AppStream 2.0 console at https://console.aws.amazon.com/appstream2.

2. On the left navigation pane, choose **User Pool** and select the users.

3. Choose **Actions, Unassign stack**.

4. Confirm the list of users in the resulting dialog box. For **Stack**, choose the desired stack. This list includes all stacks, assigned or unassigned.

5. Choose **Unassign stack**.

Disabling Users

An AppStream 2.0 administrator can disable one or more user pool users, one at a time. After being disabled, the user can no longer log in until they are re-enabled. This action does not delete the user. If the user is currently connected when an administrator disables them, their session remains active until the session cookie expires (about one hour). Stack assignments for the user are retained. If the user is re-enabled, the stack assignment becomes active again.

To disable a user

1. Open the AppStream 2.0 console at https://console.aws.amazon.com/appstream2.

2. On the left navigation pane, choose **User Pool** and select the user.

3. Choose **Actions, Disable user**.

4. Confirm the user in the resulting dialog box and choose **Disable User**.

Enabling Users

An AppStream 2.0 administrator can enable one or more user pool users, one at a time. After being enabled, the user can log in and launch applications from the stacks to which they are assigned. If the user was disabled, these assignments are retained.

To enable users

1. Open the AppStream 2.0 console at https://console.aws.amazon.com/appstream2.

2. On the left navigation pane, choose **User Pool** and select the users.

3. Choose **Actions, Enable user**.

4. Confirm the user in the resulting dialog box and choose **Enable User**.

Re-Sending Welcome Email

An AppStream 2.0 administrator can re-send the welcome email with connection instructions to user pool users. Unused passwords expire after seven days. To provide a new temporary password, the administrator must re-send the welcome email. This option is only available until the user sets their permanent password. If they've already set a password and have forgotten it, they can set a new one. For more information, see Resetting a Forgotten Password.

To resend the welcome email for a user

1. Open the AppStream 2.0 console at https://console.aws.amazon.com/appstream2.

2. On the left navigation pane, choose **User Pool** and select a user.

3. For **User Details**, choose **Resend welcome email**.

4. Confirm the success message at the top of the dashboard.

Single Sign-on Access to AppStream 2.0 Using SAML 2.0

Amazon AppStream 2.0 supports identity federation to AppStream 2.0 stacks through Security Assertion Markup Language 2.0 (SAML 2.0). You can use an identity provider (IdP) that supports SAML 2.0—such as Active Directory Federation Services (AD FS) in Windows Server, Ping One Federation Server, or Okta—to provide an onboarding flow for your AppStream 2.0 users.

This feature offers your users the convenience of one-click access to their AppStream 2.0 applications using their existing identity credentials. You also have the security benefit of identity authentication by your IdP. By using your IdP, you can control which users have access to a particular AppStream 2.0 stack.

Example Authentication Workflow

The following diagram illustrates the authentication flow between AppStream 2.0 and a third-party IdP. In this example, the administrator has set up a sign-in page to access AppStream 2.0, called `applications.exampleco.com`. The webpage uses a SAML 2.0–compliant federation service to trigger a sign-on request. The administrator has also set up a user to allow access to AppStream 2.0.

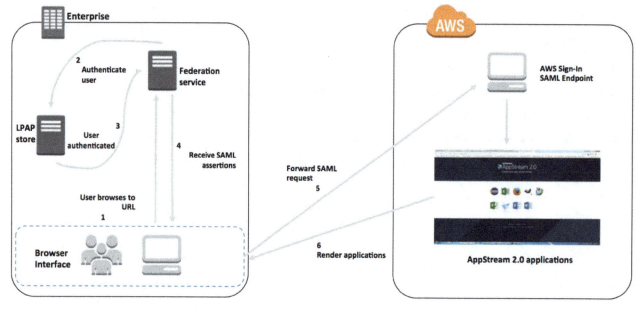

1. The user browses to `https://applications.exampleco.com`. The sign-on page requests authentication for the user.

2. The federation service requests authentication from the organization's identity store.

3. The identity store authenticates the user and returns the authentication response to the federation service.

4. On successful authentication, the federation service posts the SAML assertion to the user's browser.

5. The user's browser posts the SAML assertion to the AWS Sign-In SAML endpoint (`https://signin.aws.amazon.com/saml`). AWS Sign-In receives the SAML request, processes the request, authenticates the user, and forwards the authentication token to AppStream 2.0.

6. Using the authentication token from AWS, AppStream 2.0 authorizes the user and presents applications to the browser.

From the user's perspective, the process happens transparently: The user starts at your organization's internal portal and lands at an AppStream 2.0 application portal, without ever having to supply any AWS credentials.

Setting Up SAML

To enable users to sign in to AppStream 2.0 by using their existing credentials, and start streaming applications, you can set up identity federation using SAML 2.0. To do this, use an IAM role and a relay state URL to configure your SAML 2.0-compliant identity provider (IdP) and enable AWS to permit your federated users to access an AppStream 2.0 stack. The IAM role grants users the permissions to access the stack. The relay state is the stack portal to which users are forwarded after successful authentication by AWS.

Topics

- Prerequisites
- Step 1: Create a SAML Identity Provider in AWS IAM
- Step 2: Create a SAML 2.0 Federation IAM Role
- Step 3: Embed an Inline Policy for the IAM Role
- Step 4: Configure Your SAML-Based IdP
- Step 5: Create Assertions for the SAML Authentication Response
- Step 6: Configure the Relay State of Your Federation

Prerequisites

Complete the following prerequisites before configuring your SAML 2.0 connection.

1. Configure your SAML-based IdP to establish a trust relationship with AWS.

   - Inside your organization's network, configure your identity store to work with a SAML-based IdP. For configuration resources for using Ping Identity, Okta, Active Directory Federation Services (AD FS) in Windows Server, Shibboleth, or Google as your SAML-based IdP, see AppStream 2.0 Integration with SAML 2.0.
   - Use your SAML-based IdP to generate and download a federation metadata document that describes your organization as an IdP. This signed XML document is used to establish the relying party trust. Save this file to a location that you can access from the IAM console later.

2. Use the AppStream 2.0 management console to create an AppStream 2.0 stack. You need the stack name to create the IAM policy and to configure your IdP integration with AppStream 2.0, as described later in this topic.

   You can create an AppStream 2.0 stack by using the AppStream 2.0 management console, AWS CLI, or AppStream 2.0 API. For more information, see Create AppStream 2.0 Fleets and Stacks.

Step 1: Create a SAML Identity Provider in AWS IAM

First, create a SAML IdP in AWS IAM. This IdP defines your organization's IdP-to-AWS trust relationship using the metadata document generated by the IdP software in your organization. For more information, see Creating and Managing a SAML Identity Provider (AWS Management Console) in the *IAM User Guide*.

Step 2: Create a SAML 2.0 Federation IAM Role

Next, create a SAML 2.0 federation IAM role. This step establishes a trust relationship between IAM and your organization's IdP, which identifies your IdP as a trusted entity for federation.

To create an IAM role for the SAML IdP

1. Open the IAM console at https://console.aws.amazon.com/iam/.

2. In the navigation pane, choose **Roles, Create role**.

3. For **Role type**, choose **SAML 2.0 federation**.

4. For **SAML Provider**, select the SAML IdP that you created. **Important**
   Do not choose either of the two SAML 2.0 access level methods.

5. For **Attribute**, choose **SAML:sub_type**.

6. For **Value**, type **persistent**. This step restricts role access to only SAML user streaming requests that include a SAML subject type assertion with a value of persistent. If the SAML:sub_type is persistent, your IdP sends the same unique value for the NameID element in all SAML requests from a particular user. For more information about the SAML:sub_type assertion, see the *Uniquely Identifying Users in SAML-Based Federation* section in Using SAML-Based Federation for API Access to AWS.

7. Review your SAML 2.0 trust information, confirming the correct trusted entity and condition, and then choose **Next: Permissions**.

8. On the **Attach permissions policies** page, choose **Next: Review**. You create and embed an inline policy for this role later.

9. For **Role name**, type a name that helps you identify the purpose of this role. Because various entities might reference the role, you cannot edit the name of the role after it has been created.

10. (Optional) For **Role description**, type a description for the new role.

11. Review the role details and choose **Create role**.

Step 3: Embed an Inline Policy for the IAM Role

Next, embed an inline IAM policy for the role that you created. When you embed an inline policy, the permissions in the policy cannot be inadvertently attached to the wrong principal entity. The inline policy provides federated users with access to the AppStream 2.0 stack that you created. For information about how to embed the inline policy in JSON, see Create a Policy on the JSON Tab.

As you follow the steps in the procedure for embedding an inline policy for a user or role, note that you'll create a policy on the **JSON** tab. To do this, copy and paste the following JSON policy into the JSON window and modify the resource by entering your AWS Region Code, account ID, and stack name. In the following policy, `"Action": "appstream:Stream"` is the action that provides your AppStream 2.0 users with permissions to connect to streaming sessions on the stack that you created.

```
1  {
2    "Version": "2012-10-17",
3    "Statement": [
4      {
5        "Effect": "Allow",
6        "Action": "appstream:Stream",
7        "Resource": "arn:aws:appstream:REGION-CODE:ACCOUNT-ID-WITHOUT-HYPHENS:stack/STACK-NAME",
8        "Condition": {
9          "StringEquals": {
10            "appstream:userId": "${saml:sub}",
11            "saml:sub_type": "persistent"
12          }
13        }
14      }
15    ]
16  }
```

Choose a value for *REGION-CODE* that corresponds to the AWS Region where your AppStream 2.0 stack exists. Replace *STACK-NAME* with the name of the stack. Note that this value is case-sensitive, so the case in the stack name that you specify in this policy must match the case in the AppStream 2.0 stack name as it appears in the **Stacks** dashboard of the AppStream 2.0 management console.

Note
After you copy and paste the JSON policy, you may see an error message that indicates the validation failed. Ignore the error and continue with policy creation. You may also see an error on the **Review policy** page that indicates the policy does not grant any permissions. Ignore this error. The JSON policy is valid and provides the needed permissions.

Step 4: Configure Your SAML-Based IdP

Next, depending on your SAML-based IdP, you may need to manually update your IdP to trust AWS as a service provider by uploading the `saml-metadata.xml` file at https://signin.aws.amazon.com/static/saml-metadata.xml to your IdP. This step updates your IdP's metadata. For some IdPs, the update may already be configured. If this is the case, proceed to the next step.

If this update is not already configured in your IdP, review the documentation provided by your IdP for information about how to update the metadata. Some providers give you the option to type the URL, and the IdP obtains and installs the file for you. Others require you to download the file from the URL and then provide it as a local file.

Step 5: Create Assertions for the SAML Authentication Response

Next, depending on your SAML-based IdP, you may need to configure the information that the IdP passes as SAML attributes to AWS as part of the authentication response. For some IdPs, this information may already be configured. If this is the case, proceed to the next step.

If this information is not already configured in your IdP, provide the following:

- **SAML Subject NameID** – The unique identifier for the user who is signing in. **Note**
  For stacks with domain-joined fleets, the NameID value for the user must be provided in the format of "domain\username" using the sAMAccountName or "username@domain.com" using userPrincipalName. If you are using the sAMAccountName format, you can specify the **domain** by using either the NetBIOS name or the fully qualified domain name (FQDN). For more information, see Using Active Directory with AppStream 2.0.
- **SAML Subject Type** (with a value set to `persistent`) – Setting the value to `persistent` ensures that your IdP sends the same unique value for the `NameID` element in all SAML requests from a particular user. Make sure that your IAM policy includes a condition to only allow SAML requests with a SAML sub_type set to `persistent`, as described in Step 2: Create a SAML 2.0 Federation IAM Role.
- `Attribute` **element with the** `Name` **attribute set to** **https://aws/.amazon/.com/SAML/Attributes/Role** – This element contains one or more `AttributeValue` elements that list the IAM role and SAML IdP to which the user is mapped by your IdP. The role and IdP are specified as a comma-delimited pair of ARNs.
- `Attribute` **element with the** `SessionDuration` **attribute set to** **https://aws/.amazon/.com/SAML/Attributes/SessionDuration (optional)** – This element contains one `AttributeValue` element that specifies the maximum amount of time that a federated streaming session for a user can remain active before reauthentication is required. The default value is 60 minutes. For more information, see the *An optional Attribute element with the SessionDuration attribute set to https://aws/.amazon/.com/SAML/Attributes/SessionDuration* section in Configuring SAML Assertions for the Authentication Response.

For more information about how to configure these elements, see Configuring SAML Assertions for the Authentication Response in the *IAM User Guide*. For information about specific configuration requirements for your IdP, see the documentation for your IdP.

Step 6: Configure the Relay State of Your Federation

Finally, use your IdP to configure the relay state of your federation to point to the AppStream 2.0 stack relay state URL. After successful authentication by AWS, the user is directed to the AppStream 2.0 stack portal, defined as the relay state in the SAML authentication response.

The format of the relay state URL is as follows:

```
1  https://relay-state-region-endoint?stack=stackname&accountId=aws-account-id-without-hyphens
```

Construct your relay state URL from your AWS account ID, stack name, and the relay state endpoint associated with the region in which your stack is located.

Region	Relay state endpoint
us-east-1 (N.Virginia)	https://appstream2/.us/-east/-1/.aws/.amazon/.com/saml
us-west-2 (Oregon)	https://appstream2/.us/-west/-2/.aws/.amazon/.com/saml
ap-northeast-1 (Tokyo)	https://appstream2/.ap/-northeast/-1/.aws/.amazon/.com/saml
ap-southeast-1 (Singapore)	https://appstream2/.ap/-southeast/-1/.aws/.amazon/.com/saml
ap-southeast-2 (Sydney)	https://appstream2/.ap/-southeast/-2/.aws/.amazon/.com/saml
eu-central-1 (Frankfurt)	https://appstream2/.eu/-central/-1/.aws/.amazon/.com/saml
eu-west-1 (Ireland)	https://appstream2/.eu/-west/-1/.aws/.amazon/.com/saml

AppStream 2.0 Integration with SAML 2.0

The following links help you configure third-party SAML 2.0 identity provider solutions to work with AppStream 2.0.

IdP solution	More information
Ping Identity	Configuring an SSO connection to Amazon AppStream 2.0 — Describes how to set up single sign-on (SSO) to AppStream 2.0.
Okta	How to Configure SAML 2.0 for Amazon AppStream 2.0 — Describes how to use Okta to set up SAML federation to AppStream 2.0. For stacks that are joined to a domain, the "Application username format" must be set to "AD user principal name".
Active Directory Federation Services (AD FS) for Windows Server	Enabling Identity Federation with AD FS 3.0 and Amazon AppStream 2.0 — Describes how to provide users with SSO access to AppStream 2.0 by using their existing enterprise credentials. You can configure federated identities for AppStream 2.0 by using AD FS 3.0.
Shibboleth	Single Sign-On: Integrating AWS, OpenLDAP, and Shibboleth — Describes how to set up the initial federation between the Shibboleth IdP and the AWS Management Console. You must complete the following additional steps to enable federation to AppStream 2.0. Step 4 of the AWS Security whitepaper describes how to create IAM roles that define the permissions that federated users have to the AWS Management Console. After you create these roles and embed the inline policy as described in the whitepaper, modify this policy so that it provides federated users with permissions to access only an AppStream 2.0 stack. To do this, replace the existing policy with the policy noted in *Step 3: Embed an Inline Policy for the IAM Role*, in Setting Up SAML.When you add the stack relay state URL as described in *Step 6: Configure the Relay State of Your Federation*, in Setting Up SAML, add the relay state parameter to the federation URL as a target request attribute. For information about configuring relay state parameters, see the SAML 2.0 section in the Shibboleth documentation.
Google	Configuring Google SSO with Amazon AppStream 2.0 and Amazon AppStream 2.0 Chrome Packaging and Deployment — Describes how to set up SSO to AppStream 2.0 and how to package AppStream 2.0 as a Chrome app to improve management and deployment.

For solutions to common problems you may encounter, see Troubleshooting.

For more information about additional supported SAML providers, see Integrating Third-Party SAML Solution Providers with AWS in the *IAM User Guide*.

Using Active Directory with AppStream 2.0

You can join your Amazon AppStream 2.0 fleets and image builders to domains in Microsoft Active Directory and use your existing Active Directory domains, either cloud-based or on-premises, to launch domain-joined streaming instances. You can also use AWS Directory Service for Microsoft Active Directory, also known as Microsoft AD, to create an Active Directory domain and use that to support your AppStream 2.0 resources. For more information about using Microsoft AD, see Microsoft Active Directory in the *AWS Directory Service Administration Guide*.

By joining AppStream 2.0 to your Active Directory domain, you can:

- Allow your users and applications to access Active Directory resources such as printers and file shares from streaming sessions.
- Use Group Policy settings that are available in the Group Policy Management Console (GPMC) to define the end user experience.
- Stream applications such as Microsoft SharePoint or Microsoft Outlook that require users to be authenticated using their Active Directory login credentials.
- Apply your enterprise compliance and security policies to your AppStream 2.0 streaming instances.

Topics

- Overview of Active Directory Domains
- Before You Begin Using Active Directory with AppStream 2.0
- Tutorial: Setting Up Active Directory
- AppStream 2.0 Active Directory Administration
- More Info

Overview of Active Directory Domains

Using Active Directory domains with AppStream 2.0 requires an understanding of how they work together and the configuration tasks that you'll need to complete. You'll need to complete the following tasks:

1. Configure Group Policy settings as needed to define the end user experience and security requirements for applications.

2. Create the domain-joined application stack in AppStream 2.0.

3. Create the AppStream 2.0 application in the SAML 2.0 identity provider and assign it to end users either directly or through Active Directory groups.

For your users to be authenticated to a domain, several steps must occur when these users initiate an AppStream 2.0 streaming session. The following diagram illustrates the end-to-end user authentication flow from the initial browser request through SAML and Active Directory authentication.

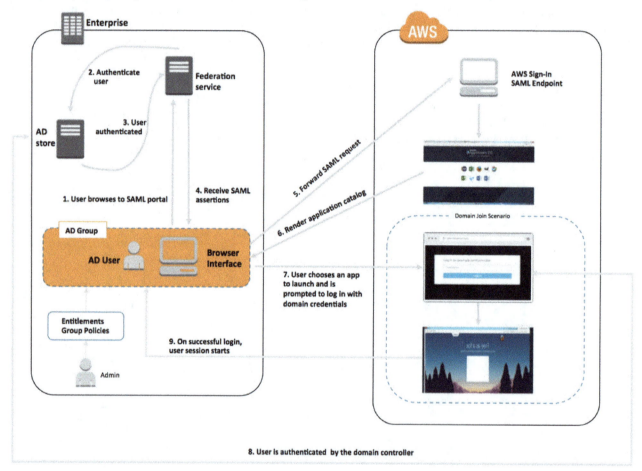

User Authentication Flow

1. The user browses to `https://applications.exampleco.com`. The sign-on page requests authentication for the user.

2. The federation service requests authentication from the organization's identity store.

3. The identity store authenticates the user and returns the authentication response to the federation service.

4. On successful authentication, the federation service posts the SAML assertion to the user's browser.

5. The user's browser posts the SAML assertion to the AWS Sign-In SAML endpoint (`https://signin.aws.amazon.com/saml`). AWS Sign-In receives the SAML request, processes the request, authenticates the user, and forwards the authentication token to the AppStream 2.0 service.

6. Using the authentication token from AWS, AppStream 2.0 authorizes the user and presents applications to the browser.

7. The user chooses an application and is prompted to enter login information for the domain.

8. The domain controller is contacted for user authentication.

9. After being authenticated with the domain, the user's session starts with domain connectivity.

From the user's perspective, the process happens transparently. The user starts at your organization's internal portal and lands at an AppStream 2.0 application portal, without having to enter AWS credentials. Only Active Directory domain login credentials are required.

Before a user can initiate this process, you must configure Active Directory with the required entitlements and Group Policy settings and create a domain-joined application stack.

Before You Begin Using Active Directory with AppStream 2.0

Before you use Microsoft Active Directory domains with AppStream 2.0, be aware of the following requirements.

Requirements

- You need a Microsoft Active Directory domain to which to join your streaming instances. If you don't have an Active Directory domain or you want to use your on-premises Active Directory environment, see Active Directory Domain Services on the AWS Cloud: Quick Start Reference Deployment.

- You need a domain service account with permissions to create and manage computer objects in the domain that you intend to use with AppStream 2.0. For information, see How to Create a Domain Account in Active Directory in the Microsoft documentation.

  When you associate this Active Directory domain with AppStream 2.0, provide the service account name and password. AppStream 2.0 uses this account to create and manage computer objects in the directory. For more information, see Granting Permissions to Create and Manage Active Directory Computer Objects.

- When you register your Active Directory domain with AppStream 2.0, you must provide an organizational unit (OU) distinguished name. Create an OU for this purpose. The default Computers container is not an OU and cannot be used by AppStream 2.0. For more information, see Finding the Organizational Unit Distinguished Name.

- The directories that you plan to use with AppStream 2.0 must be accessible through their fully qualified domain names (FQDNs) through the virtual private cloud (VPC) in which your streaming instances are launched. For more information, see Active Directory and Active Directory Domain Services Port Requirements in the Microsoft documentation.

- SAML 2.0-based user federation is required for application streaming from domain-joined fleets. You cannot launch sessions to domain-joined instances by using CreateStreamingURL or the AppStream 2.0 User Pool.

- You must use an image that supports joining image builders and fleets to an Active Directory domain. All public images published on or after July 24, 2017 support joining an Active Directory domain. For more information, see Amazon AppStream 2.0 Windows Image Version History and Tutorial: Setting Up Active Directory.

Tutorial: Setting Up Active Directory

To use Active Directory with AppStream 2.0, you must first register your directory configuration by creating a Directory Config object in AppStream 2.0. This object includes the information required to join streaming instances to an Active Directory domain. You create a Directory Config object by using the AppStream 2.0 management console, AWS SDK, or AWS CLI. You can then use your directory configuration to launch domain-joined fleets and image builders.

Topics

- Step 1: Create a Directory Config Object
- Step 2: Create an Image by Using a Domain-Joined Image Builder
- Step 3: Create a Domain-Joined Fleet
- Step 4: Configure SAML 2.0

Step 1: Create a Directory Config Object

The Directory Config object that you create in AppStream 2.0 will be used in later steps.

If you are using the AWS SDK, you can use the CreateDirectoryConfig operation. If you are using the AWS CLI, you can use the create-directory-config command.

To create a Directory Config object by using the AppStream 2.0 console

1. Open the AppStream 2.0 console at https://console.aws.amazon.com/appstream2.

2. In the navigation pane, choose **Directory Configs**, **Create Directory Config**.

3. For **Directory Name**, provide the fully qualified domain name (FQDN) of the Active Directory domain (for example, `corp.example.com`). Each region can have only one **Directory Config** value with a specific directory name.

4. For **Service Account Name**, enter the name of an account that can create computer objects and that has permissions to join the domain. For more information, see Granting Permissions to Create and Manage Active Directory Computer Objects. The account name must be in the format `DOMAIN\username`.

5. For **Password** and **Confirm Password**, type the directory password for the specified account.

6. For **Organizational Unit (OU)**, type the distinguished name of at least one OU for streaming instance computer objects. The default Computers container is not an OU and cannot be used by AppStream 2.0. For more information, see Finding the Organizational Unit Distinguished Name.

7. To add more than one OU, select the plus sign (+) next to **Organizational Unit (OU)**. To remove OUs, choose the **x** icon.

8. Choose **Next**.

9. Review the configuration information and choose **Create**.

Step 2: Create an Image by Using a Domain-Joined Image Builder

Next, using the AppStream 2.0 image builder, create a new image with Active Directory domain-join capabilities. Note that the fleet and image can be members of different domains. You join the image builder to a domain to enable domain join and to install applications. Fleet domain join is discussed in the next section.

To create an image for launching domain-joined fleets

1. Follow the procedures in Tutorial: Create a Custom Image.

2. For the base image selection step, use an AWS base image released on or after July 24, 2017. For a current list of released AWS images, see Amazon AppStream 2.0 Windows Image Version History.

3. For **Step 3: Configure Network**, select a VPC and subnets with network connectivity to your Active Directory environment. Select the security groups that are set up to allow access to your directory through your VPC subnets.

4. Also in **Step 3: Configure Network**, expand the **Active Directory Domain (Optional)** section, and select values for the **Directory Name** and **Directory OU** to which the image builder should be joined.

5. Review the image builder configuration and choose **Create**.

6. Wait for the new image builder to reach a **Running** state, and choose **Connect**.

7. Log in to the image builder in Administrator mode or as a directory user with local administrator permissions. For more information, see Granting Local Administrator Rights on Image Builders.

8. Complete the steps in Tutorial: Create a Custom Image to install applications and create a new image.

Step 3: Create a Domain-Joined Fleet

Using the private image created in the previous step, create an Active Directory domain-joined fleet for streaming applications. The domain can be different than the one that you used for the image builder to create the image.

To create a domain-joined fleet

1. Follow the procedures in Create a Fleet.

2. For the image selection step, use the image that was created in the previous step, Step 2: Create an Image by Using a Domain-Joined Image Builder.

3. For **Step 4: Configure Network**, select a VPC and subnets with network connectivity to your Active Directory environment. Select the security groups that are set up to allow communication to your domain.

4. Also in **Step 4: Configure Network**, expand the **Active Directory Domain (Optional)** section and select the values for the **Directory Name** and **Directory OU** to which the fleet should be joined.

5. Review the fleet configuration and choose **Create**.

6. Complete the remaining steps in Create AppStream 2.0 Fleets and Stacks so that your fleet is associated with a stack and running.

Step 4: Configure SAML 2.0

Your users must use your SAML 2.0-based identity federation environment to launch streaming sessions from your domain-joined fleet.

To configure SAML 2.0 for single sign-on access

1. Follow the procedures in Setting Up SAML.

2. AppStream 2.0 requires that the SAML_Subject `NameID` value for the user who is logging in be provided in either of the following formats:

   - `domain\username` using the sAMAccountName
   - `username@domain.com` using the userPrincipalName

   If you are using the sAMAccountName format, you can specify the `domain` by using either the NetBIOS name or the fully qualified domain name (FQDN).

3. Provide access to your Active Directory users or groups to enable access to the AppStream 2.0 stack from your identity provider application portal.

4. Complete the remaining steps in Setting Up SAML.

To log in a user with SAML 2.0

1. Log in to your SAML 2.0 provider's application catalog and open the AppStream 2.0 SAML application that you created in the previous procedure.

2. When the AppStream 2.0 application catalog is displayed, select an application to launch.

3. When a loading icon is displayed, you are prompted to provide a password. The domain user name provided by your SAML 2.0 identity provider appears above the password field. Enter your password, and choose **log in**.

The streaming instance performs the Windows login procedure, and the selected application opens.

AppStream 2.0 Active Directory Administration

Setting up and using Active Directory with AppStream 2.0 involves the following administrative tasks.

Topics

- Granting Permissions to Create and Manage Active Directory Computer Objects
- Finding the Organizational Unit Distinguished Name
- Granting Local Administrator Rights on Image Builders
- Updating the Service Account Used for Joining the Domain
- Locking the Streaming Session When the User is Idle
- Editing the Directory Configuration
- Deleting a Directory Configuration
- Configuring AppStream 2.0 to Use Domain Trusts
- Managing AppStream 2.0 Computer Objects in Active Directory

Granting Permissions to Create and Manage Active Directory Computer Objects

To allow AppStream 2.0 to perform Active Directory computer object operations, you need an account with sufficient permissions. As a best practice, use an account that has only the minimum privileges necessary. The minimum Active Directory organizational unit (OU) permissions are as follows:

- Create Computer Object
- Change Password
- Reset Password
- Write Description

Before setting up permissions, you'll need to do the following first:

- Obtain access to a computer or an EC2 instance that is joined to your domain.
- Install the Active Directory User and Computers MMC snap-in. For more information, see Installing or Removing Remote Server Administration Tools for Windows 7 in the Microsoft documentation.
- Log in as a domain user with appropriate permissions to modify the OU security settings.
- Create or identify the user account, service account, or group for which to delegate permissions.

To set up minimum permissions

1. Open **Active Directory Users and Computers** in your domain or on your domain controller.

2. In the left navigation pane, select the first OU on which to provide domain join privileges, open the context (right-click) menu , and then choose **Delegate Control**.

3. On the **Delegation of Control Wizard** page, choose **Next**, **Add**.

4. For **Select Users, Computers, or Groups**, select the pre-created user account, service account, or group, and then choose **OK**.

5. On the **Tasks to Delegate** page, choose **Create a custom task to delegate**, and then choose **Next**.

6. Choose **Only the following objects in the folder, Computer objects**.

7. Choose **Create selected objects in this folder, Next**.

8. For **Permissions**, choose **Read, Write, Change Password, Reset Password, Next**.

9. On the **Completing the Delegation of Control Wizard** page, verify the information and choose **Finish**.

10. Repeat steps 2-9 for any additional OUs that require these permissions.

If you delegated permissions to a group, create a user or service account with a strong password and add that account to the group. This account will then have sufficient privileges to connect your streaming instances to the directory. Use this account when creating your AppStream 2.0 directory configuration.

Finding the Organizational Unit Distinguished Name

When you register your Active Directory domain with AppStream 2.0, you must provide an organizational unit (OU) distinguished name. Create an OU for this purpose. The default Computers container is not an OU and cannot be used by AppStream 2.0. The following procedure shows how to obtain this name.

Note
The distinguished name must start with **OU=** or it cannot be used for computer objects.

Before you complete this procedure, you'll need to do the following first:

- Obtain access to a computer or an EC2 instance that is joined to your domain.
- Install the Active Directory User and Computers MMC snap-in. For more information, see Installing or Removing Remote Server Administration Tools for Windows 7 in the Microsoft documentation.
- Log in as a domain user with appropriate permissions to read the OU security properties.

To find the distinguished name of an OU

1. Open **Active Directory Users and Computers** in your domain or on your domain controller.

2. Under **View**, ensure that **Advanced Features** is enabled.

3. In the left navigation pane, select the first OU to use for AppStream 2.0 streaming instance computer objects, open the context (right-click) menu, and then choose **Properties**.

4. Choose **Attribute Editor**.

5. Under **Attributes**, for **distinguishedName**, choose **View**.

6. For **Value**, select the distinguished name, open the context menu, and then choose **Copy**.

Granting Local Administrator Rights on Image Builders

By default, Active Directory domain users do not have local administrator rights on image builder instances. You can grant these rights by using Group Policy preferences in your directory, or manually, by using the local administrator account on an image builder. Granting local administrator rights to a domain user allows that user to install applications on and create images in an AppStream 2.0 image builder.

Topics

- Using Group Policy preferences
- Using the local Administrators group on the image builder

Using Group Policy preferences

You can use Group Policy preferences to grant local administrator rights to Active Directory users or groups and to all computer objects in the specified OU. The Active Directory users or groups to which you want to grant local administrator permissions must already exist. To use Group Policy preferences, you'll need to do the following first:

- Obtain access to a computer or an EC2 instance that is joined to your domain.
- Install the Group Policy Management Console (GPMC) MMC snap-in. For more information, see Installing or Removing Remote Server Administration Tools for Windows 7 in the Microsoft documentation.
- Log in as a domain user with permissions to create Group Policy objects (GPOs). Link GPOs to the appropriate OUs.

To use Group Policy preferences to grant local administrator permissions

1. In your directory or on a domain controller, open the command prompt as an administrator, type `gpmc.msc`, and then press ENTER.

2. In the left console tree, select the OU where you will create a new GPO or use an existing GPO, and then do either of the following:

   - Create a new GPO by opening the context (right-click) menu and choosing **Create a GPO in this domain, Link it here**. For **Name**, provide a descriptive name for this GPO.
   - Select an existing GPO.

3. Open the context menu for the GPO, and choose **Edit**.

4. In the console tree, choose **Computer Configuration**, **Preferences**, **Windows Settings**, **Control Panel Settings**, and **Local Users and Groups**.

5. Select **Local Users and Groups** selected, open the context menu , and choose **New**, **Local Group**.

6. For **Action**, choose **Update**.

7. For **Group name**, choose **Administrators (built-in)**.

8. Under **Members**, choose **Add...** and specify the Active Directory user accounts or groups to which to assign local administrator rights on the streaming instance. For **Action**, choose **Add to this group**, and choose **OK**.

9. To apply this GPO to other OUs, select the additional OU, open the context menu and choose **Link an Existing GPO**.

10. Using the new or existing GPO name that you specified in step 2, scroll to find the GPO, and then choose **OK**.

11. Repeat steps 9 and 10 for additional OUs that should have this preference.

12. Choose **OK** to close the **New Local Group Properties** dialog box.

13. Choose **OK** again to close the GPMC.

To apply the new preference to the GPO, you must stop and restart any running image builders or fleets. The Active Directory users and groups that you specified in step 8 are automatically granted local administrator rights on the image builders and fleets in the OU to which the GPO is linked.

Using the local Administrators group on the image builder

To grant Active Directory users or groups local administrator rights on your image builder, you can manually add these users or groups to the local Administrators group on the image builder. Image builders that are created from images with these rights maintain the same rights.

The Active Directory users or groups to which to grant local administrator rights must already exist.

To add Active Directory users or groups to the local Administrators group on the image builder

1. Open the AppStream 2.0 console at https://console.aws.amazon.com/appstream2.

2. Connect to the image builder in Administrator mode. The image builder must be running and domain-joined. For more information, see Tutorial: Setting Up Active Directory.

3. Choose **Start**, **Administrative Tools**, and then double-click **Computer Management**.

4. In the left navigation pane, choose **Local Users and Groups** and open the **Groups** folder.

5. Open the **Administrators** group and choose **Add...**.

6. Select all Active Directory users or groups to which to assign local administrator rights and choose **OK**. Choose **OK** again to close the **Administrator Properties** dialog box.

7. Close Computer Management.

8. To log in as an Active Directory user and test whether that user has local administrator rights on the image builder, choose **Admin Commands**, **Switch user**, and then enter the credentials of the relevant user.

Updating the Service Account Used for Joining the Domain

To update the service account that AppStream 2.0 uses for joining the domain, we recommend using two separate service accounts for joining image builders and fleets to your Active Directory domain. Using two separate service accounts ensures that there is no disruption in service when a service account needs to be updated (for example, when a password expires).

To update a service account

1. Create an Active Directory group and delegate the correct permissions to the group.

2. Add your service accounts to the new Active Directory group.

3. When needed, edit your AppStream 2.0 Directory Config object by entering the user name and password for the new service account.

After you've set up the Active Directory group with the new service account, any new streaming instance operations will use the new service account, while in-process streaming instance operations continue to use the old account without interruption.

The service account overlap time while the in-process streaming instance operations complete is very short, no more than a day. The overlap time is needed because you shouldn't delete or change the password for the old service account during the overlap period, or existing operations can fail.

Locking the Streaming Session When the User is Idle

AppStream 2.0 relies on a setting that you configure in the GPMC to lock the streaming session after your user is idle for specified amount of time. To use the GPMC, you'll need to do the following first:

- Obtain access to a computer or an EC2 instance that is joined to your domain.
- Install the GPMC. For more information, see Installing or Removing Remote Server Administration Tools for Windows 7 in the Microsoft documentation.
- Log in as a domain user with permissions to create GPOs. Link GPOs to the appropriate OUs.

To automatically lock the streaming instance when your user is idle

1. In your directory or on a domain controller, open the command prompt as an administrator, type `gpmc.msc`, and then press ENTER.

2. In the left console tree, select the OU where you will create a new GPO or use an existing GPO, and then do either of the following:
   - Create a new GPO by opening the context (right-click) menu and choosing **Create a GPO in this domain, Link it here**. For **Name**, provide a descriptive name for this GPO.
   - Select an existing GPO.

3. Open the context menu for the GPO, and choose **Edit**.

4. Under **User Configuration**, expand **Policies**, **Administrative Templates**, **Control Panel**, and then choose **Personalization**.

5. Double-click **Enable screen saver**.

6. In the **Enable screen saver** policy setting, choose **Enabled**.

7. Choose **Apply**, and then choose **OK**.

8. Double-click **Force specific screen saver**.

9. In the **Force specific screen saver** policy setting, choose **Enabled**.

10. Under **Screen saver executable name**, enter **scrnsave.scr**. When this setting is enabled, the system displays a black screen saver on the user's desktop.

11. Choose **Apply**, and then choose **OK**.

12. Double-click **Password protect the screen saver**.

13. In the **Password protect the screen saver** policy setting, choose **Enabled**.

14. Choose **Apply**, and then choose **OK**.

15. Double-click **Screen saver timeout**.

16. In the **Screen saver timeout** policy setting, choose **Enabled**.

17. For **Seconds**, specify the length of time that users must be idle before the screen saver is applied. To set the idle time to 10 minutes, specify 600 seconds.

18. Choose **Apply**, and then choose **OK**.

19. In the console tree, under **User Configuration**, expand **Policies**, **Administrative Templates**, **System**, and then choose **Ctrl+Alt+Del Options**.

20. Double-click **Remove Lock Computer**.

21. In the **Remove Lock Computer** policy setting, choose **Disabled**.

22. Choose **Apply**, and then choose **OK**.

Editing the Directory Configuration

After a AppStream 2.0 directory configuration has been created, you can edit it to add, remove, or modify organizational units, update the service account username, or update the service account password.

To update a directory configuration

1. Open the AppStream 2.0 console at https://console.aws.amazon.com/appstream2.

2. In the left navigation pane, choose **Directory Configs** and select the directory configuration to edit.

3. Choose **Actions**, **Edit**.

4. Update the fields to be changed. To add additional OUs, select the plus sign (+) next to the topmost OU field. To remove an OU field, select the **x** next to the field. **Note**
At least one OU is required. OUs that are currently in use cannot be removed.

5. To save changes, choose **Update Directory Config**.

6. The information in the **Details** tab should now update to reflect the changes.

Changes to the service account user name and password do not impact in-process streaming instance operations. New streaming instance operations use the updated credentials. For more information, see Updating the Service Account Used for Joining the Domain.

Deleting a Directory Configuration

You can delete an AppStream 2.0 directory configuration that is no longer needed. Directory configurations that are associated with any image builders or fleets cannot be deleted.

To delete a directory configuration

1. Open the AppStream 2.0 console at https://console.aws.amazon.com/appstream2.

2. In the left navigation pane, choose **Directory Configs** and select the directory configuration to delete.

3. Choose **Actions, Delete**.

4. Verify the name in the pop-up message, and choose **Delete**.

5. Choose **Update Directory Config**.

Configuring AppStream 2.0 to Use Domain Trusts

AppStream 2.0 supports Active Directory domain environments where network resources such as file servers, applications, and computer objects reside in one domain, and the user objects reside in another. The domain service account used for computer object operations does not need to be in the same domain as the AppStream 2.0 computer objects.

When creating the directory configuration, specify a service account that has the appropriate permissions to manage computer objects in the Active Directory domain where the file servers, applications, computer objects and other network resources reside.

Your end user Active Directory accounts must have the "Allowed to Authenticate" permissions for the following:

- AppStream 2.0 computer objects
- Domain controllers for the domain

For more information, see Granting Permissions to Create and Manage Active Directory Computer Objects.

Managing AppStream 2.0 Computer Objects in Active Directory

AppStream 2.0 does not delete computer objects from Active Directory. These computer objects can be easily identified in your directory. Each computer object in the directory is created with the `Description` attribute, which specifies a fleet or an image builder instance and the name.

Computer Object Description Examples

Type	Name	Description Attribute
Fleet	ExampleFleet	`AppStream 2.0 - fleet:` `ExampleFleet`

Image builder	ExampleImageBuilder	`AppStream 2.0 -`
		`image-builder:`
		`ExampleImageBuilder`

You can identify and delete inactive computer objects created by AppStream 2.0 by using the following `dsquery computer` and `dsrm` commands. For more information, see Dsquery computer and Dsrm in the Microsoft documentation.

The `dsquery` command identifies inactive computer objects over a certain period of time and uses the following format. The `dsquery` command should also be run with the parameter `-desc "AppStream 2.0*"` to display only AppStream 2.0 objects.

```
1 dsquery computer "OU-distinguished-name" -desc "AppStream 2.0*" -inactive number-of-weeks-since-
    last-login
```

- OU-distinguished-name is the distinguished name of the organizational unit. For more information, see Finding the Organizational Unit Distinguished Name. If you don't provide the *OU-distinguished-name* parameter, the command searches the entire directory.
- number-of-weeks-since-last-log-in is the desired value based on how you want to define inactivity.

For example, the following command displays all computer objects in the OU=ExampleOU,DC=EXAMPLECO,DC=COM organizational unit that have not been logged into within the past two weeks.

```
1 dsquery computer OU=ExampleOU,DC=EXAMPLECO,DC=COM -desc "AppStream 2.0*" -inactive 2
```

If any matches are found, the result is one or more object names. The dsrm command deletes the specified object and uses the following format:

```
1 dsrm objectname
```

Where objectname is the full object name from the output of the dsquery command. For example, if the dsquery command above results in a computer object named "ExampleComputer", the dsrm command to delete it would be as follows:

```
1 dsrm "CN=ExampleComputer,OU=ExampleOU,DC=EXAMPLECO,DC=COM"
```

You can chain these commands together by using the pipe (|) operator. For example, to delete all AppStream 2.0 computer objects, prompting for confirmation for each, use the following format. Add the -noprompt parameter to dsrm to disable confirmation.

```
1 dsquery computer OU-distinguished-name -desc "AppStream 2.0*" -inactive number-of-weeks-since-
    last-log-in | dsrm
```

More Info

For more information related to this topic, see the following resources:

- Troubleshooting Notification Codes—Resolutions to notification code errors.
- Troubleshooting Active Directory Domain Join—Help with common difficulties.
- Microsoft Active Directory—Information about using AWS Directory Service.

Monitoring Amazon AppStream 2.0 Resources

AppStream 2.0 publishes metrics to Amazon CloudWatch to enabled detailed tracking and deep dive analysis. These statistics are recorded for an extended period so you can access historical information and gain a better perspective on how your fleets are performing. For more information, see the Amazon CloudWatch User Guide.

Viewing Fleet Usage Using the Console

You can monitor Amazon AppStream 2.0 using the AppStream 2.0 console or the CloudWatch console.

To view fleet usage in the AppStream 2.0 console

1. Open the AppStream 2.0 console at https://console.aws.amazon.com/appstream2.

2. In the left pane, choose **Fleets**.

3. Select a fleet and choose its **Fleet Usage** tab.

4. By default, the graph displays the following metrics: `ActualCapacity`, `InUseCapacity`, and `CapacityUtilization`. You can select additional metrics to graph or change the period.

To view fleet usage in the CloudWatch console

1. Open the CloudWatch console at https://console.aws.amazon.com/cloudwatch/.

2. In the left pane, choose **Metrics**.

3. Choose the **AppStream** namespace and then choose **Fleet Metrics**.

4. Select the metrics to graph.

AppStream 2.0 Metrics and Dimensions

Amazon AppStream 2.0 sends the following metrics and dimension information to Amazon CloudWatch.

Amazon AppStream 2.0 Metrics

AppStream 2.0 sends metrics to CloudWatch one time every minute. The `AWS/AppStream` namespace includes the following metrics.

Metric	Description
ActualCapacity	The total number of instances that are available for streaming or are currently streaming. ActualCapacity = AvailableCapacity + InUseCapacity Units: Count Valid statistics: Average, Minimum, Maximum
AvailableCapacity	The number of idle instances currently available for user sessions. AvailableCapacity = ActualCapacity - InUseCapacity Units: Count Valid statistics: Average, Minimum, Maximum

Metric	Description
CapacityUtilization	The percentage of instances in a fleet that are being used, using the following formula. CapacityUtilization = (InUseCapacity/ActualCapacity) * 100 Monitoring this metric helps with decisions about increasing or decreasing the value of a fleet's desired capacity. Units: Percent Valid statistics: Average, Minimum, Maximum
DesiredCapacity	The total number of instances that are either running or pending. This represents the total number of concurrent streaming sessions your fleet can support in a steady state. DesiredCapacity = ActualCapacity + PendingCapacity Units: Count Valid statistics: Average, Minimum, Maximum
InUseCapacity	The number of instances currently being used for streaming sessions. One `InUseCapacity` count represents one streaming session. Units: Count Valid statistics: Average, Minimum, Maximum
PendingCapacity	The number of instances being provisioned by AppStream 2.0. Represents the additional number of streaming sessions the fleet can support after provisioning is complete. When provisioning starts, it usually takes 10-20 minutes for an instance to become available for streaming. Units: Count Valid statistics: Average, Minimum, Maximum
RunningCapacity	The total number of instances currently running. Represents the number of concurrent streaming sessions that can be supported by the fleet in its current state. This metric is provided for Always-On fleets only, and has the same value as the `ActualCapacity` metric. Units: Count Valid statistics: Average, Minimum, Maximum
InsufficientCapacityError	The number of session requests rejected due to lack of capacity. You can set alarms to use this metric to be notified of users waiting for streaming sessions. Units: Count Valid statistics: Average, Minimum, Maximum, Sum

Dimensions for Amazon AppStream 2.0 Metrics

To filter the metrics provided by Amazon AppStream 2.0, use the following dimension.

Dimension	Description
Fleet	The name of the fleet.

Controlling Access to Amazon AppStream 2.0 with IAM Policies and Service Roles

AWS Identity and Access Management (IAM) policies grant permissions to specific resources and API actions. To manage AppStream 2.0 resources and perform API actions through the AWS Command Line Interface (AWS CLI), AWS SDK, or AWS Management Console, you must have the permissions defined in the AmazonAppStreamFullAccess managed policy.

If you sign into the AppStream 2.0 console as an IAM user, you must attach this policy to your IAM user account. If you sign in through console federation, you must attach this policy to the IAM role that was used for federation.

The AmazonAppStreamReadOnlyAccess managed policy is available for users who require only read access to AppStream 2.0 resources.

Topics

- IAM Service Roles Required for Managing AppStream 2.0 Resources
- Permissions Required for IAM Service Role Creation
- Checking for the AmazonAppStreamServiceAccess Service Role and Policies
- Checking for the ApplicationAutoScalingForAmazonAppStreamAccess Service Role and Policies
- Application Auto Scaling Required IAM Permissions
- IAM Policies and the Amazon S3 Bucket for Home Folders

IAM Service Roles Required for Managing AppStream 2.0 Resources

In addition to having the permissions defined in the AmazonAppStreamFullAccess policy, you must also have the AmazonAppStreamServiceAccess and the ApplicationAutoScalingForAmazonAppStreamAccess IAM service roles present in your AWS account, with the appropriate policies attached. The AppStream 2.0 and Application Auto Scaling services assume these roles and call other AWS services as needed to manage your resources.

AmazonAppStreamServiceAccess
While AppStream 2.0 resources are being created, the AppStream 2.0 service makes API calls to other AWS services on your behalf by assuming this role. If this service role is not present in your AWS account and the required IAM permissions and trust relationship policies are not attached, you cannot create AppStream 2.0 fleets.

ApplicationAutoScalingForAmazonAppStreamAccess
The Application Auto Scaling service uses this service role to scale AppStream 2.0 resources on your behalf. If this service role is not present in your AWS account and the required IAM permissions and trust relationship policies are not attached, you cannot scale AppStream 2.0 fleets.

Permissions Required for IAM Service Role Creation

If you have the required permissions, these two service roles are automatically created by AppStream 2.0, with the required IAM policies attached, when you get started with the AppStream 2.0 service in an AWS Region. You or an administrator must have one of the following permissions to get started with AppStream 2.0 in your AWS account:

- Permissions to create an IAM role and attach IAM policies to a role
- AdministratorAccess permissions

Note
IAM roles and policies control which AppStream 2.0 resources can be accessed. The user pool controls access to AppStream 2.0 itself. For more information, see Manage Access Using the AppStream 2.0 User Pool.

Checking for the AmazonAppStreamServiceAccess Service Role and Policies

Follow the steps in this section to check whether the AmazonAppStreamServiceAccess service role is present and has the correct policies attached. If this service role is not present and must be created, you or an administrator with the required permissions must perform the steps to get started with AppStream 2.0 in your AWS account.

Topics

- AmazonAppStreamServiceAccess permissions policy
- AmazonAppStreamServiceAccess trust relationship policy

To check whether the AmazonAppStreamServiceAccess IAM service role is present

1. Open the IAM console at https://console.aws.amazon.com/iam/.

2. In the navigation pane, choose **Roles**.

3. In the search box, type `amazonappstreamservice` to narrow the list of roles to select, and then choose **AmazonAppStreamServiceAccess**. If this role is listed, select it to view the role summary.

4. On the **Permissions** tab, confirm whether the AmazonAppStreamServiceAccess permissions policy is attached and follows the correct format. If so, the permissions policy is correctly configured.

5. On the **Trust relationships** tab, choose **Edit trust relationship**, and then confirm whether the AmazonAppStreamServiceAccess trust relationship policy is attached and follows the correct format. If so, the trust relationship is correctly configured. Choose **Cancel** and close the IAM console.

AmazonAppStreamServiceAccess permissions policy

The format for this permissions policy is as follows:

```
1  {
2    "Version": "2012-10-17",
3    "Statement": [
4      {
5        "Effect": "Allow",
6        "Action": [
7          "ec2:DescribeVpcs",
8          "ec2:DescribeSubnets",
9          "ec2:DescribeAvailabilityZones",
10         "ec2:CreateNetworkInterface",
11         "ec2:DescribeNetworkInterfaces",
12         "ec2:DeleteNetworkInterface",
13         "ec2:DescribeSubnets",
14         "ec2:AssociateAddress",
15         "ec2:DisassociateAddress",
16         "ec2:DescribeRouteTables",
17         "ec2:DescribeSecurityGroups"
18       ],
19       "Resource": "*"
20     },
21     {
22       "Effect": "Allow",
23       "Action": [
24         "s3:CreateBucket",
25         "s3:ListBucket",
26         "s3:GetObject",
27         "s3:PutObject",
```

```
28      "s3:DeleteObject",
29      "s3:GetObjectVersion",
30      "s3:DeleteObjectVersion",
31      "s3:PutBucketPolicy"
32    ],
33    "Resource": "arn:aws:s3:::appstream2-36fb080bb8-*"
34   }
35  ]
36 }
```

AmazonAppStreamServiceAccess trust relationship policy

The format for this trust relationship policy is as follows:

```
1  {
2    "Version": "2012-10-17",
3    "Statement": [
4      {
5        "Effect": "Allow",
6        "Principal": {
7        "Service": "appstream.amazonaws.com"
8        },
9        "Action": "sts:AssumeRole"
10     }
11   ]
12 }
```

Checking for the ApplicationAutoScalingForAmazonAppStreamAccess Service Role and Policies

Follow the steps in this section to check whether the ApplicationAutoScalingForAmazonAppStreamAccess service role is present and has the correct policies attached. If this service role is not present and must be created, you or an administrator with the required permissions must perform the steps to get started with AppStream 2.0 in your AWS account.

Topics

- ApplicationAutoScalingForAmazonAppStreamAccess permissions policy
- ApplicationAutoScalingForAmazonAppStreamAccess trust relationship policy

To check whether the ApplicationAutoScalingForAmazonAppStreamAccess IAM service role is present

1. Open the IAM console at https://console.aws.amazon.com/iam/.

2. In the navigation pane, choose **Roles**.

3. In the search box, type `applicationautoscaling` to narrow the list of roles to select, and then choose **ApplicationAutoScalingForAmazonAppStreamAccess**. If this role is listed, select it to view the role summary.

4. On the **Permissions** tab, confirm whether the ApplicationAutoScalingForAmazonAppStreamAccess permissions policy is attached and follows the correct format. If so, the permissions policy is correctly configured.

5. On the **Trust relationships **tab, choose **Edit trust relationship**, and then confirm whether the ApplicationAutoScalingForAmazonAppStreamAccess trust relationship policy is attached and follows the correct format. If so, the trust relationship is correctly configured. Choose **Cancel** and close the IAM console.

ApplicationAutoScalingForAmazonAppStreamAccess permissions policy

The format for this permissions policy is as follows:

```
1  {
2    "Version": "2012-10-17",
3    "Statement": [
4      {
5        "Effect": "Allow",
6        "Action": [
7          "appstream:UpdateFleet",
8          "appstream:DescribeFleets"
9        ],
10       "Resource": [
11         "*"
12       ]
13     },
14     {
15       "Effect": "Allow",
16       "Action": [
17         "cloudwatch:DescribeAlarms"
18       ],
19       "Resource": [
20         "*"
21       ]
22     }
23   ]
24 }
```

ApplicationAutoScalingForAmazonAppStreamAccess trust relationship policy

The format for this trust relationship policy is as follows:

```
1  {
2    "Version": "2012-10-17",
3    "Statement": [
4      {
5        "Effect": "Allow",
6        "Principal": {
7          "Service": "application-autoscaling.amazonaws.com"
8        },
9        "Action": "sts:AssumeRole"
10     }
11   ]
12 }
```

Application Auto Scaling Required IAM Permissions

To use AppStream 2.0 Fleet Auto Scaling, the IAM user accessing fleet creation and scaling settings must have appropriate permissions for the services that support dynamic scaling. AppStream 2.0 requires the following permissions:

```
1  {
2    "Version": "2012-10-17",
3    "Statement": [
4      {
5        "Effect": "Allow",
6        "Action": [
7            "appstream:*",
8            "application-autoscaling:*",
9            "cloudwatch:DeleteAlarms",
10           "cloudwatch:DescribeAlarmsForMetric",
11           "cloudwatch:DisableAlarmActions",
12           "cloudwatch:DescribeAlarms",
13           "cloudwatch:EnableAlarmActions",
14           "cloudwatch:ListMetrics",
15           "cloudwatch:PutMetricAlarm",
16           "iam:passrole",
17           "iam:ListRoles"
18        ],
19        "Resource": "*"
20      }
21    ]
22  }
```

IAM Policies and the Amazon S3 Bucket for Home Folders

Access to the Amazon S3 bucket for home folders is managed using IAM permissions and policies.

Topics

- Deleting the Amazon S3 Bucket for Home Folders
- Restricting Administrator Access to the Amazon S3 Bucket for Home Folders

Deleting the Amazon S3 Bucket for Home Folders

AppStream 2.0 adds an Amazon S3 bucket policy that prevents the accidental deletion of the S3 bucket, shown at the end of this section. You must delete the S3 bucket policy first, and then you can delete the S3 bucket. For more information, see Deleting or Emptying a Bucket in the *Amazon Simple Storage Service Developer Guide*.

```
1  {
2    "Version": "2012-10-17",
3    "Statement": [
4      {
5        "Sid": "PreventAccidentalDeletionOfBucket",
6        "Effect": "Deny",
7        "Principal": "*",
8        "Action": "s3:DeleteBucket",
9        "Resource": "arn:aws:s3:::appstream2-36fb080bb8-region-code-account-id-without-hyphens"
10     }
11   ]
```

```
12 }
```

Restricting Administrator Access to the Amazon S3 Bucket for Home Folders

By default, administrators who can access the Amazon S3 bucket created by AppStream 2.0 can view and modify content that is part of users' home folders. To restrict administrator access to the S3 bucket containing user files, we recommend applying the S3 bucket access policy based on the following template:

```
1  {
2    "Sid": "RestrictedAccess",
3    "Effect": "Deny",
4    "NotPrincipal":
5    {
6      "AWS": [
7        "arn:aws:iam::account:role/service-role/AmazonAppStreamServiceAccess",
8        "arn:aws:sts::account:assumed-role/AmazonAppStreamServiceAccess/PhotonSession",
9        "arn:aws:iam::account:user/IAM-user-name"
10      ]
11    },
12      "Action": "s3:*",
13      "Resource": "arn:aws:s3:::appstream2-36fb080bb8-region-account"
14    }
15  ]
16  }
```

This policy allows home folder S3 bucket access only to the users specified and to the AppStream 2.0 service. For every IAM user who should have access, replicate the following line:

```
1  "arn:aws:iam::account:user/IAM-user-name"
```

In the following example, the policy restricts access to the home folder S3 bucket for anyone other than IAM users marymajor and johnstiles, and also restricts access to the AppStream 2.0 service, in AWS Region us-west-2 for account ID 123456789012.

```
1  {
2    "Sid": "RestrictedAccess",
3    "Effect": "Deny",
4    "NotPrincipal":
5    {
6      "AWS": [
7        "arn:aws:iam::123456789012:role/service-role/AmazonAppStreamServiceAccess",
8        "arn:aws:sts::123456789012:assumed-role/AmazonAppStreamServiceAccess/PhotonSession",
9        "arn:aws:iam::123456789012:user/marymajor",
10        "arn:aws:iam::123456789012:user/johnstiles"
11      ]
12    },
13      "Action": "s3:*",
14      "Resource": "arn:aws:s3:::appstream2-36fb080bb8-us-west-2-123456789012"
15    }
16  ]
17  }
```

Tagging Your Amazon AppStream 2.0 Resources

AWS enables you to assign metadata to your AWS resources in the form of tags. You can use these tags to help manage your AppStream 2.0 image builders, images, fleets, and stacks, and also organize data, including billing data.

You can:

- Logically group resources in different ways (for example, by purpose, owner, or environment).

  This is useful when you have many resources of the same type.

- Quickly identify a specific resource based on the tags that you've assigned to it

- Identify and control AWS costs

For example, you can identify and group AppStream 2.0 fleets that are in different environments (such as Development or Production) or that are assigned to different business units (such as HR or Marketing). You can then track the associated AWS costs for these fleets on a detailed level. To do this, sign up to get your AWS account bill with tag key values included. For more information about setting up a cost allocation report with tags, see Monthly Cost Allocation Report in the *AWS Billing and Cost Management User Guide*.

Topics

- Tagging Basics
- Tag Restrictions
- Working with Tags in the AppStream 2.0 Console
- Working with Tags by Using the AppStream 2.0 API, an AWS SDK, or AWS CLI

Tagging Basics

Tags consist of a key-value pair, similar to other AWS services tags. To tag a resource, you specify a *key* and a *value* for each tag. A key can be a general category, such as "project", "owner", or "environment", with specific associated values, and you can share the same key and value across multiple resources. You can tag an AppStream 2.0 resource immediately after you create it or later on. If you delete a resource, the tags are removed from that resource on deletion. However, other AppStream 2.0 and AWS resources that have the same tag key are not impacted.

You can edit tag keys and values, and you can remove tags from a resource at any time. You can set the value of a tag to an empty string, but you can't set the name of a tag to null. If you add a tag that has the same key as an existing tag on that resource, the new value overwrites the old value. If you delete a resource, any tags for the resource are also deleted.

Note
If you plan to set up a monthly cost allocation report to track AWS costs for AppStream 2.0 resources, keep in mind that tags added to existing AppStream 2.0 resources appear in your cost allocation report on the first of the following month for resources that are renewed in that month.

Tag Restrictions

- The maximum number of tags per AppStream 2.0 resource is 50.
- The maximum key length is 128 Unicode characters in UTF-8.
- The maximum value length is 256 Unicode characters in UTF-8.
- Tag keys and values are case-sensitive.
- Do not use the "aws:" prefix in your tag names or values because it is a system tag that is reserved for AWS use. You cannot edit or delete tag names or values with this prefix. Tags with this prefix do not count against your tags per resource limit.

- You can only use the following special characters: $+ - = . \_ : / @$.
- Although you can share the same key and value across multiple resources, you cannot have duplicate keys on the same resource.
- Tags can only be added to resources that are already created (you cannot specify tags on resource creation).

Working with Tags in the AppStream 2.0 Console

You can add, edit, and delete tags for existing resources by using the AppStream 2.0 console.

To add, edit, or delete tags for an existing AppStream 2.0 resource

1. Open the AppStream 2.0 console at https://console.aws.amazon.com/appstream2.

2. From the navigation bar, select the region that contains the resource for which you want to add, edit, or delete tags.

3. In the navigation pane, select the resource type. The resource type can be an image builder, image, fleet, or stack.

4. Select the resource from the resource list.

5. Choose **Tags**, **Add/Edit Tags**, and then do one or more of the following:
   - To add a tag, choose **Add Tag**, and then specify the key and value for each tag.
   - To edit a tag, modify the key and value for the tag as needed.
   - To delete a tag, choose the **Delete** icon (X) for the tag.

6. Choose **Save**.

Working with Tags by Using the AppStream 2.0 API, an AWS SDK, or AWS CLI

If you're using the AppStream 2.0 API, an AWS SDK or the AWS Command Line Interface (CLI), you can use the following AppStream 2.0 actions to add, edit, remove, or list tags for your resources:

Task	AWS CLI	API Action
Add or overwrite one or more tags for a resource.	tag-resource	TagResource
Remove one or more tags for a resource.	untag-resource	UntagResource
List one or more tags for a resource.	list-tags-for-resource	ListTagsForResource

When you use the AppStream 2.0 API, an AWS SDK, or AWS CLI actions to add, edit, remove, or list tags for an AppStream 2.0 resource, specify the resource by using its Amazon Resource Name (ARN). An ARN uniquely identifies an AWS resource and uses the following general syntax.

```
1  arn:aws:appstream:region:account:resourceType/resourceName
```

region
The AWS Region in which the resource was created (for example, `us-east-1`).

account
The AWS account ID, with no hyphens (for example, `123456789012`).

resourceType
The type of resource. You can tag the following AppStream 2.0 resource types: `image-builder`, `image`, `fleet`, and `stack`.

resourceName
The name of the resource.

For example, you can obtain the ARN for an AppStream 2.0 fleet by using the AWS CLI describe-fleets command. Copy the following command.

```
1 aws appstream describe-fleets
```

For an environment that contains a single fleet named `TestFleet`, the ARN for this resource would appear in the JSON output similar to the following.

```
1 "Arn": "arn:aws:appstream:us-east-1:123456789012:fleet/TestFleet"
```

After you obtain the ARN for this resource, you can add two tags by using the tag-resource command:

```
1 aws appstream tag-resource --resource arn:awsappstream:us-east-1:123456789012:fleet/TestFleet --
    tags Environment=Test,Department=IT
```

The first tag, `Environment=Test`, indicates that the fleet is in a test environment. The second tag, `Department=IT`, indicates that the fleet is in the IT department.

You can use the following command to list the two tags that you added to the fleet.

```
1 aws appstream list-tags-for-resource --resource arn:aws:appstream:us-east-1:123456789012:fleet/
    TestFleet
```

For this example, the JSON output appears as follows:

```
1 {
2     "Tags": {
3         "Environment" : "Test",
4         "Department" : "IT"
5     }
6 }
```

Troubleshooting

If you encounter difficulties when working with Amazon AppStream 2.0, consult the following troubleshooting resources.

Topics

- General Troubleshooting
- Troubleshooting Image Builders
- Troubleshooting Fleets
- Troubleshooting Active Directory Domain Join
- Troubleshooting Notification Codes

General Troubleshooting

The following are possible general issues you might have while using Amazon AppStream 2.0.

Topics

- SAML federation is not working. The user is not authorized to view AppStream 2.0 applications.
- After federating from an ADFS portal, my streaming session doesn't start. I am getting the error "Sorry connection went down".
- I get an invalid redirect URI error.
- My stack's home folders aren't working correctly.
- My users can't access their home folder directory from one of our applications.

SAML federation is not working. The user is not authorized to view AppStream 2.0 applications.

This might happen because the inline policy that is embedded for the SAML 2.0 federation IAM role does not include permissions to the stack ARN. The IAM role is assumed by the federated user who is accessing an AppStream 2.0 stack. Edit the role permissions to include the stack ARN. For more information, see Single Sign-on Access to AppStream 2.0 Using SAML 2.0 and Troubleshooting SAML 2.0 Federation with AWS in the *IAM User Guide*.

After federating from an ADFS portal, my streaming session doesn't start. I am getting the error "Sorry connection went down".

Set the claim rule's **Incoming Claim Type** for the **NameID** SAML attribute to **UPN** and try the connection again.

I get an invalid redirect URI error.

This error occurs due to a malformed or invalid AppStream 2.0 stack relay state URL. Make sure that the relay state configured in your federation setup is the same as the stack relay state that is displayed in the stack details through the AppStream 2.0 console. If they are the same and the problem still persists, contact AWS Support. For more information, see Single Sign-on Access to AppStream 2.0 Using SAML 2.0.

My stack's home folders aren't working correctly.

Problems with home folder backup to an S3 bucket can occur in the following scenarios:

- There is no internet connectivity from the streaming instance, or there is no access to the private Amazon S3 VPC endpoint, if applicable.
- Network bandwidth consumption is too high. For example, multiple large files are being downloaded or streamed by the user while the service is trying to back up a home folder that contains large files to Amazon S3.
- An administrator deleted the bucket created by the service.
- An administrator incorrectly edited the Amazon S3 permissions for the **AmazonAppStreamServiceAccess** service role.

For more information, see the Amazon Simple Storage Service Console User Guide and Amazon Simple Storage Service Developer Guide.

My users can't access their home folder directory from one of our applications.

Some applications do not recognize the redirect that displays the home folder as a top-level folder in File Explorer. If this is the case, your users can access their home folder from within an application during a streaming session by choosing **File Open** from the application interface and browsing to the following directory: C:\Users\PhotonUser\My Files\Home Folder.

Troubleshooting Image Builders

The following are possible issues you might have while using Amazon AppStream 2.0 image builders.

Topics

- I cannot connect to the internet from my image builder.
- When I tried installing my application, I see an error that the operating system version is not supported.
- When I connect to my image builder, I see a login screen asking me to enter Ctrl+Alt+Delete to log in. However, my local machine intercepts the key strokes.
- When I switched between admin and test modes, I saw a request for a password. I don't know how to get a password.
- I get an error when I add my installed application.
- I accidentally quit a background service on the image builder and got disconnected. I am now unable to connect to that image builder.
- The application fails to launch in test mode.
- The application could not connect to a network resource in my VPC.
- I customized my image builder desktop, but my changes are not available when connecting to a session after launching a fleet from the image I created.
- My application is missing a command line parameter when launching.
- I am unable to use my image with a fleet after installing an antivirus application.
- My image creation failed.

I cannot connect to the internet from my image builder.

Image builders cannot communicate to the internet by default. To resolve this issue, launch your image builder in a VPC subnet that has internet access. You can enable internet access from your VPC subnet using a NAT gateway. Alternatively, you can configure an internet gateway in your VPC, and attach an Elastic IP address to your image builder. For more information, see Network Settings for Amazon AppStream 2.0 .

When I tried installing my application, I see an error that the operating system version is not supported.

Only applications that can be installed on Windows Server 2012 R2 can be added to an AppStream 2.0 image. Check if your application is supported on Microsoft Windows Server 2012 R2.

When I connect to my image builder, I see a login screen asking me to enter Ctrl+Alt+Delete to log in. However, my local machine intercepts the key strokes.

Your client may intercept certain key combinations locally instead of sending them to the image builder session. To reliably send the **Ctrl+Alt+Delete** key combination to the image builder, choose **Admin Commands**, **Send Ctrl+Alt+Delete**. The **Admin Commands** menu is available on the top right corner of the image builder session toolbar.

When I switched between admin and test modes, I saw a request for a password. I don't know how to get a password.

AppStream 2.0 usually logs you into the user mode that you choose automatically. On some occasions, the switch may not happen automatically. If a password is requested, choose **Admin Commands**, **Log me in**. This sends a one-time password, securely, to your image builder and pastes it into the **Password** field.

I get an error when I add my installed application.

Check if your application type is supported. You can add applications of the types `.exe`, `.lnk`, and `.bat`.

Check if your application is installed under the `C:\Users` folder hierarchy. Any application installed under `C:\Users` is not supported. Select a different installation folder under `C:\` when installing the application.

I accidentally quit a background service on the image builder and got disconnected. I am now unable to connect to that image builder.

Try stopping the image builder, restarting it and connecting to it again. If the problem persists, you must launch (create) a new image builder. Do not stop any background services running on the image builder instance. Doing so may interrupt your image builder session or interfere with the image creation.

The application fails to launch in test mode.

Check if your application requires elevated user privileges or any special permissions that are usually available only to an administrator. The **Image Builder Test** mode has the same limited permissions on the image builder instance as your end users have on an AppStream 2.0 test fleet. If your applications require elevated permissions, they do not launch in the **Image Builder Test** mode.

The application could not connect to a network resource in my VPC.

Check if the image builder was launched in the correct VPC subnet. You may also need to verify that the route tables in your VPC are configured to allow a connection.

I customized my image builder desktop, but my changes are not available when connecting to a session after launching a fleet from the image I created.

Changes that are saved as part of a local user session, such as time settings, are not persisted when creating an image. To persist any local user session changes, add them to the local group policy on the image builder instance.

My application is missing a command line parameter when launching.

You can provide a command line parameter when using image builder to add an application to an image. If the launch parameters for the application do not change for each user, you can enter them while adding an application to the image in the image builder instance.

If the launch parameters are different for every launch, you can pass them programmatically when using the `CreateStreamingURL` API. Set the `sessionContext` and `applicationID` parameters in the API fields. The sessionContext is included as a command line option when launching the application.

If the launch parameters must be computed on the fly, you can launch your application using a script. You can parse the `sessionContext` parameter within your script before launching your application with a computed parameter.

I am unable to use my image with a fleet after installing an antivirus application.

You can install any tools, including antivirus programs, on your AppStream 2.0 stack by using the image builder before creating an image. However, these programs should not block any network ports or stop any processes that are used by the AppStream 2.0 service. We recommend testing your application in **Image Builder Test** mode before creating an image and attempting to use it with a fleet.

My image creation failed.

Verify that you did not make any changes to AppStream 2.0 services before starting the image creation. Try creating your image again; if it fails, contact AWS Support. For more information, see AWS Support Center.

Troubleshooting Fleets

The following are possible issues that might occur when users connect to streaming sessions launched from fleet instances.

Topics

- My applications won't work correctly unless I use the Internet Explorer defaults. How do I restore the Internet Explorer default settings?
- I need to persist environment variables across my fleet instances.
- I want to change the default Internet Explorer home page for my users.
- When my users end a streaming session and then start a new one, they see a message that says no streaming resources are available.

My applications won't work correctly unless I use the Internet Explorer defaults. How do I restore the Internet Explorer default settings?

If your AppStream 2.0 environment includes applications that render elements, you might need to restore the Internet Explorer default settings to enable full enable access to the internet.

To automatically restore the Internet Explorer default settings

1. Open the AppStream 2.0 console at https://console.aws.amazon.com/appstream2.

2. In the left navigation pane, choose **Images**, **Image Builder**.

3. Choose the image builder on which to restore the Internet Explorer default settings, verify that it is in the **Running** state, and choose **Connect**.

4. Log in to the image builder by doing either of the following:

   - If your image builder is not joined to an Active Directory domain, on the **Local User** tab, choose **Template User**.
   - If your image builder is joined to an Active Directory domain, choose the **Directory User** tab, enter the credentials for a domain user that does not have local administrator permissions on the image builder, then choose **Log in**.

5. Open Internet Explorer and reset your settings by doing the following:

   1. In the upper right area of the Internet Explorer browser window, choose the **Tools** icon, then choose **Internet options**.

   2. Choose the **Advanced **tab, then choose **Reset**.

   3. When prompted to confirm your choice, choose **Reset** again.

   4. When the **Reset Internet Explorer Settings** message displays, choose **Close**.

6. In the upper right area of the image builder desktop, choose **Admin Commands**, **Switch User**.

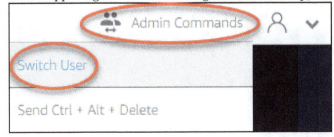

7. This disconnects your current session and opens the login menu. Do either of the following:

- If your image builder is not joined to an Active Directory domain, on the **Local User** tab, choose **Administrator**.
- If your image builder is joined to an Active Directory domain, choose the **Directory User** tab, and log in as a domain user who has local administrator permissions on the image builder.

8. On the image builder desktop, open Image Assistant.

9. Follow the necessary steps in Image Assistant to finish creating your image. For more information, see Tutorial: Create a Custom Image.

I need to persist environment variables across my fleet instances.

Environment variables enable you to dynamically pass settings across applications. You can make user environment variables and system environment variables available across your fleet instances. You can also create environment variables with limited scope, which is useful when you need to use the same environment variable with different values across different applications. For more information, see Persist Environment Variables.

I want to change the default Internet Explorer home page for my users.

You can use Group Policy to set the default home page in Internet Explorer for your users. You can also enable users to change the default page that you set. For more information, see Change the Default Internet Explorer Home Page for Users' Streaming Sessions.

When my users end a streaming session and then start a new one, they see a message that says no streaming resources are available.

When a user ends a session, AppStream 2.0 terminates the underlying instance and creates a new instance if needed to meet the desired capacity of the fleet. If a user tries to start a new session before AppStream 2.0 creates the new instance and all other instances are in use, the user will receive an error stating that no streaming resources are available. If your users start and stop sessions frequently, consider increasing your fleet capacity. For more information, see Fleet Auto Scaling for Amazon AppStream 2.0. Or, consider increasing the maximum session duration for your fleet and instructing your users to close their browser during periods of inactivity rather than ending their session.

Troubleshooting Active Directory Domain Join

The following are possible issues you might have while setting up and using Active Directory with Amazon AppStream 2.0. For help troubleshooting notification codes, see Troubleshooting Notification Codes.

Topics

- My image builders and fleet instances are stuck in the PENDING state.
- My users aren't able to log in with the SAML application.
- My fleet instances work for one user but don't cycle correctly.
- My user Group Policy objects aren't applying successfully.
- My AppStream 2.0 streaming instances aren't joining the Active Directory domain.
- User login is taking a long time to complete on a domain-joined streaming session.
- The changes I made in the image builder aren't reflected in end user streaming sessions.
- My users can't access a domain resource in a domain-joined streaming session but they can access the resource from a domain-joined image builder.

My image builders and fleet instances are stuck in the PENDING state.

Image builders and fleet instances can take up to 25 minutes to move into a ready state and become available. If your instances are taking longer than 25 minutes to become available, in Active Directory, verify whether new computer objects were created in the correct organizational units (OUs). If there are new objects, the streaming instances will be available soon. If the objects aren't there, check the directory configuration details in your AppStream 2.0 Directory Config: Directory name (the fully qualified domain name of the directory, service account username and password, and the OU distinguished name.

Image builder and fleet errors are displayed in the AppStream 2.0 console on the **Notifications** tab for the fleet or image builder. Fleet errors are also available using the AppStream 2.0 API via the DescribeFleets operation, or the CLI command describe-fleets.

My users aren't able to log in with the SAML application.

AppStream 2.0 relies on the SAML_Subject "NameID" attribute from your identity provider to populate the username field to log in your user. The username can either be formatted as "domain\username", or "user@domain.com". If you are using "domain\username" format, domain can either be the NetBIOS name or the fully qualified domain name. If using "user@domain.com" format, the UserPrincipalName attribute can be used. If you've verified your SAML_Subject attribute is configured correctly and the problem persists, contact AWS Support. For more information, see AWS Support Center.

My fleet instances work for one user but don't cycle correctly.

Fleet instances are cycled after a user completes a session, ensuring that each user has a new instance. When the cycled fleet instance is brought online, it joins the domain using the computer name of the previous instance. To ensure that this operation happens successfully, the service account requires **Change Password** and **Reset Password** permissions on the organizational unit (OU) to which the computer object is joining. Check the service account permissions and try again. If the problem persists, contact AWS Support. For more information, see AWS Support Center.

My user Group Policy objects aren't applying successfully.

By default, computer objects apply computer-level policies based on the OU in which the computer object resides, while applying user-level policies based on the OU in which the user resides. If your user-level policies aren't being applied, you can do one of the following:

- Move the user-level policies to the OU in which the user Active Directory object resides
- Enable computer-level "loopback processing," which applies the user-level policies in the computer object OU.

For more information, see Loopback processing of Group Policy at Microsoft Support.

My AppStream 2.0 streaming instances aren't joining the Active Directory domain.

The Active Directory domain to use with AppStream 2.0 must be accessible through its fully qualified domain name (FQDN) via the VPC in which your streaming instances are launched.

To test that your domain is accessible

1. Launch an Amazon EC2 instance in the same VPC, subnet, and security groups that you use with AppStream 2.0.

2. Manually join the EC2 instance to your Active Directory domain using the FQDN (for example, `yourdomain.exampleco.com`) with the service account that you intend to use with AppStream 2.0. Use the following command in a Windows PowerShell console:

```
1 netdom join computer /domain:FQDN /OU:path /ud:user /pd:password
```

If this manual join fails, proceed to the next step.

3. If you cannot manually join to your domain, open a command prompt and verify that you can resolve the FQDN using the `nslookup` command. For example:

```
1 nslookup yourdomain.exampleco.com
```

Successful name resolution returns a valid IP address. If you are unable to resolve your FQDN, you may need to update your VPC DNS servers by using a DHCP option set for your domain. Then, come back to this step. For more information, see DHCP Options Sets in the *Amazon VPC User Guide*.

4. If the FQDN resolves, validate connectivity by using the following `telnet` command.

```
1 telnet yourdomain.exampleco.com 389
```

A successful connection shows a blank command prompt window without any connection errors. You may need to install the Telnet Client feature on your EC2 instance. For more information, see Install Telnet Client in the Microsoft documentation.

If you were not able to manually join the EC2 instance to your domain, but were successful in resolving the FQDN and testing connectivity with the Telnet Client, your VPC security groups may be preventing access. Active Directory requires certain network port settings. For more information, see Active Directory and Active Directory Domain Services Port Requirements in the Microsoft documentation.

User login is taking a long time to complete on a domain-joined streaming session.

AppStream 2.0 performs a Windows login action after the end user provides their domain password, and then launches the application after successful authentication. The login and launch time is impacted by many variables, such as network contention to the domain controllers or time taken to apply group policies to the streaming instance. If domain authentication takes too long to complete, try the following actions.

- Minimize the network latency from your AppStream 2.0 region to your domain controllers by choosing the correct domain controllers. For example, if your fleet is in us-east-1, use domain controllers with high bandwidth and low latency to us-east-1 through Active Directory Sites and Services zone mappings. For more information, see Active Directory Sites and Services in the Microsoft documentation.

- Ensure that your group policies and user login scripts don't take prohibitively long to apply or execute.

If your login to AppStream 2.0 fails after 3 minutes with a message "An unknown error occurred," validate that your group policies are not restricting third-party credential providers. There are two policies that block AppStream 2.0 from authenticating your domain users:

- **Computer Configuration > Administrative Templates > Windows Components > Windows Logon Options > Disable or Enable software Secure Attention Sequence** — This policy should be set to **Enabled** for **Services**.
- **Computer Configuration > Administrative Templates > System > Logon > Exclude credential providers** — Ensure that the following CLSID is *not* listed: `e7c1bab5-4b49-4e64-a966-8 d99686f8c7c`

The changes I made in the image builder aren't reflected in end user streaming sessions.

User-specific settings in the image builder are saved in the specific user profile, and do not persist to the streaming instances. Examples include drive mounting, wallpaper changes, browser customizations, or Internet Explorer customizations. You need to manage these settings using the Microsoft Active Directory Group Policy settings that are applied to the OUs under which your streaming instances are created.

To quickly test whether your Group Policy settings are applied to the end user, connect to your image builder, login as a domain user and test the experience. For more information, see Group Policy for Beginners in the Microsoft documentation.

My users can't access a domain resource in a domain-joined streaming session but they can access the resource from a domain-joined image builder.

Confirm that your fleet is created in the same VPC, subnets, and security groups as your image builder, and that your user has the appropriate permissions to access and use the domain resource.

Troubleshooting Notification Codes

The following are notification codes and resolution steps for notifications you may see while setting up and using Amazon AppStream 2.0. These notifications can be found in the **Notifications** tab in the AppStream 2.0 console, after selecting an image builder or fleet. Fleet notifications can also be obtained using the AppStream 2.0 API operation DescribeFleets, or using the describe-fleets CLI command.

Active Directory Domain Join

The following are notification codes and resolution steps for codes you might encounter while setting up and using Active Directory with Amazon AppStream 2.0.

DOMAIN_JOIN_ERROR_ACCESS_DENIED
Message: Access is denied.
Resolution: The service account specified in the directory configuration does not have permissions to create the computer object, or reuse an existing one. Validate the permissions and start the image builder or fleet. For more information, see Granting Permissions to Create and Manage Active Directory Computer Objects.

DOMAIN_JOIN_ERROR_LOGON_FAILURE
Message: The username or password is incorrect.
Resolution: The service account specified in the directory configuration has an invalid username or password. Update the configuration and re-create the image builder or fleet that had the error.

DOMAIN_JOIN_NERR_PASSWORD_EXPIRED
Message: The password of this user has expired.
Resolution: The password for the service account specified in the AppStream 2.0 directory configuration has expired. Change the password for the service account in your Active Directory domain, then update the configuration, and re-create the image builder or fleet that had the error.

DOMAIN_JOIN_ERROR_DS_MACHINE_ACCOUNT_QUOTA_EXCEEDED
Message: Your computer could not be joined to the domain. You have exceeded the maximum number of computer accounts you are allowed to create in this domain. Contact your system administrator to have this limit reset or increased.
Resolution: The service account specified on the directory configuration does not have permissions to create the computer object, or reuse an existing one. Validate the permissions and start the image builder or fleet. For more information, see Granting Permissions to Create and Manage Active Directory Computer Objects.

DOMAIN_JOIN_ERROR_INVALID_PARAMETER
Message: A parameter is incorrect. This error is returned if the LpName parameter is NULL or the NameType parameter is specified as NetSetupUnknown or an unknown nametype.
Resolution: This error can occur when the distinguished name for the OU is incorrect. Validate the OU chosen. If you continue to encounter this error, contact AWS Support. For more information, see AWS Support Center.

DOMAIN_JOIN_ERROR_MORE_DATA
Message: More data is available.
Resolution: This error can occur when the distinguished name for the OU is incorrect. Validate the OU chosen. If you continue to encounter this error, contact AWS Support. For more information, see AWS Support Center.

DOMAIN_JOIN_ERROR_NO_SUCH_DOMAIN
Message: The specified domain either does not exist or could not be contacted.
Resolution: The streaming instance was unable to contact your Active Directory domain. To ensure network connectivity, confirm your VPC, subnet, and security group settings. For more information, see My AppStream 2.0 streaming instances aren't joining the Active Directory domain..

DOMAIN_JOIN_NERR_WORKSTATION_NOT_STARTED
Message: The Workstation service has not been started.
Resolution: An error occurred starting the Workstation service. Ensure that the service is enabled in your

image. If you continue to encounter this error, contact AWS Support. For more information, see AWS Support Center.

DOMAIN_JOIN_ERROR_NOT_SUPPORTED

Message: The request is not supported. This error is returned if a remote computer was specified in the lpServer parameter and this call is not supported on the remote computer.

Resolution: Contact AWS Support for assistance. For more information, see AWS Support Center.

DOMAIN_JOIN_ERROR_FILE_NOT_FOUND

Message: The system cannot find the file specified.

Resolution: This error occurs when an invalid organizational unit (OU) distinguished name is provided. The distinguished name must start with **OU=**. Validate the OU distinguished name and try again. For more information, see Finding the Organizational Unit Distinguished Name.

Amazon AppStream 2.0 Service Limits

By default, AWS limits the resources that you can create and the number of users who can use the service. To request a limit increase, use the AppStream 2.0 Limits form.

The following table lists the limits for each AppStream 2.0 resource. Where no default limit is listed for a specific instance family or instance type, the limit is 0.

Default Limits Per AWS Region Per Account

Resource	Default Limit
Stacks	5
Fleets	5
Fleet instances	[See the AWS documentation website for more details]
Image builder instances	[See the AWS documentation website for more details]
Images	5
Concurrent image copies	2 per destination region
Image copies (per month)	20

Document History for Amazon AppStream 2.0

The following table describes important changes to the documentation for Amazon AppStream 2.0.

- **API version:** 2016-12-01

Regional settings and default application and Windows settings	Created Enable Regional Settings for Your AppStream 2.0 Users and updated Tutorial: Create a Custom Image and other content as needed.	June 14, 2018
Google Drive support	Created Enable and Administer Google Drive for Your AppStream 2.0 Users and updated other content as needed.	June 4, 2018
Administrative controls for data transfer	Updated Create AppStream 2.0 Fleets and Stacks and other content as needed.	May 24, 2018
New region	Updated Setting Up SAML to add one new AppStream 2.0 region: Frankfurt.	March 28, 2018
Custom branding	Created Add Your Custom Branding to Amazon AppStream 2.0 and updated other content as needed.	March 26, 2018
Image copy	Updated Tutorial: Create a Custom Image and other content as needed.	February 23, 2018
New regions	Updated Setting Up SAML to add two new AppStream 2.0 regions: Singapore and Sydney.	January 24, 2018
Resource tagging	Created Tagging Your Amazon AppStream 2.0 Resources and updated other content as needed.	December 15, 2017
Managed AppStream 2.0 agent updates	Created Amazon AppStream 2.0 Agent Version History and updated other content as needed.	December 7, 2017
On-Demand fleets	Created Fleet Type and updated other content as needed.	September 19, 2017
Instance families	Created AppStream 2.0 Instance Families and updated other content as needed.	July 25, 2017
Active Directory	Created Using Active Directory with AppStream 2.0 and updated other content as needed.	July 24, 2017
User pool	Created Manage Access Using the AppStream 2.0 User Pool and updated other content as needed.	June 15, 2017

Security groups	Created Security Groups and updated other content as needed.	May 26, 2017
Home folders	Created Home Folders and VPC Endpoints and updated other content as needed.	May 18, 2017
Default internet access	Created Network Settings for Amazon AppStream 2.0 and updated other content as needed.	April 21, 2017
Fleet automatic scaling	Created Fleet Auto Scaling for Amazon AppStream 2.0 and updated other content as needed.	March 23, 2017
Fleet management	Created Amazon AppStream 2.0 Fleets and Stacks and updated other content as needed.	February 22, 2017
SAML 2.0 support	Created Single Sign-on Access to AppStream 2.0 Using SAML 2.0 and updated other content as needed.	February 15, 2017
Image builders	Created AppStream 2.0 Image Builders and updated other content as needed.	January 19, 2017
Initial release	Created this guide.	December 01, 2016